Marilyn
At French River

~~∾o∾~~

and
Other Ghostly Sightings

Marilyn
At French River

~o~

and
Other Ghostly Sightings

Terry Boyle

~o~

Polar Bear Press
Toronto

Marilyn at French River:
And Other Ghostly Sightings

For information, contact Polar Bear Press, 35 Prince Andrew Place, Toronto, Ontario M3C 2H2

Polar
Bear
Press

Canadian Cataloguing in Publication Data

Boyle, Terry, 1945-
 Marilyn at French River: And Other Ghostly Sighting/ Terry Boyle

includes index.
ISBN 1-896757-18-9

1. Haunted Places – Ontario – I Title.

BF1472.C3B69 2003   133.1'09713   C2002-900802-6

Cover photo of Marilyn Monroe, Private Collection

Other books by Terry Boyle

FIT TO BE TIED:
Ontario's Murderous Past

FULL MOONS & BLACK CATS:
Everyday Rules to Guide You Life

HAUNTED ONTARIO:
Ghostly inns, hotels and other eerie places
you can visit

HAUNTED ONTARIO 2:
More spine-tingling encounters in places
you can visit

Polar
Bear
Press

distributed by
North 49 Books
35 Prince Andrew Place
Toronto, Ontario M3C 2H2
416 449-4000

NORTH
49
BOOKS

Table of Contents

Introduction

To see a ghost is to believe in ghosts. The people I have interviewed over the years are no longer skeptical. Sometimes they're not sure of what exactly they 'saw' but you cannot tell them that they did not see anything. They were not dreaming or hallucinating— they know what they have seen or experienced.

Hans Holzer, a well-respected lecturer in parapsychology and the author of 119 books on ghosts, haunted places and parapsychology defines a ghost as "a surviving emotional memory of someone who died traumatically or tragically, but is unaware of his or her death. Unwilling to part with the physical world, those human personalities stay on at the spot where their tragedy or their emotional attachment existed prior to their physical death."

Ghosts, he believes are electromagnetic fields originally encased in an outer layer called the physical body. According to Holzer, "After death that outer layer dissolves, leaving the inner self free. With the majority of people, this inner self—also referred to as the soul or the psyche—will drift out into the nonphysical world where it is able to move forward and backward in time and space, motivated by thought and possessed of all earth memories fully intact."

People who hear or see ghostly phenomena are, by that definition, psychic. They are people who have the ability to tune in on the refined vibrations or electromagnetic field after it leaves the physical body. There are many, many people with this ability although they may be unaware of the gift or not always in touch with it. You do not have to be a professional medium to believe in ghosts or to actually see one.

I encourage everyone who reads this book to venture to these places to get their own sensing. All of these sites are inhabited by one or more spirits. I have been to every one and my own ability is growing through my research. I hope you enjoy this book as much as I've enjoyed exploring these ghostly places.

This book would have not been possible without the help of the many people who so graciously agreed to be interviewed.

Terry Boyle
November 2002
Parry Sound, Ont.

A Grave Visit to the Grafton Inn

A woman searches about empty rooms and narrow hallways in the Grafton Village Inn. She is searching for a place to rest. She glides up the central staircase and enters the second floor ballroom. Her attention is drawn to a window overlooking the quiet main street. For a brief moment she glances outside before her gaze settles on the windowsill. A tear drops onto a fractured slab of misplaced limestone resting on the ledge. The word 'Fran' is visible on the slab. In that moment she fades from sight. The Grafton Village Inn, it seems, has a permanent guest.

Driving east along Highway 2 last summer, I reached the small village of Grafton and first saw the Inn. Somehow I knew a spirit haunted that building. I turned around and parked across from the Inn. I crossed the street, opened the front door and walked in. I promptly asked the first waitress I saw if the place was haunted. "Oh yes," she

A portion of Fran's headstone, discovered in the basement of the Grafton Village Inn.

replied. "Come with me." Up the stairs we went to look at—a tombstone.

My hunch was right.

At one time Grafton could boast no fewer than six inns. United Empire Loyalists, mainly from Vermont and Massachusetts, settled the village itself around 1798. British and Irish immigrants followed closely behind.

The settlement was known as Haldimond Corners, named after Sir Frederick Haldimond, a Swiss-born citizen later to become Governor-in-Chief of Upper Canada between 1778 and 1786.

In March of 1832 the village was renamed Grafton in honour of the former home of resident John Grover from Vermont.

In November of 1833, the *Cobourg Star* newspaper printed an excerpt from a letter by a visitor to the Inn, "Our respected host, Mr Pepper, late of Grovers Inn has taken possession of this beautiful new establishment, the Mansion House. A sign has just been elevated displaying the British Arms in bold relief under which are emblazoned the national emblem. His table we found well supplied with substantials, not forgetting the luxuries which have ever distinguished it."

John Arklands purchased the Inn in 1835 and operated it until 1855 when it was purchased by Benjamin Brown. Three years later Brown severed a portion, 58 feet x 58 feet (or 19m x 19m), from the hotel lot and sold it to the Municipal Council of Haldimond for the township building site.

In 1892 Michael Mulhall bought the Inn and there he raised a family of 12 children. Mulhall severed the west side of the property for the site of the Haldimond Telephone System. The Mulhalls sold the establishment in 1921 and it then had several owners. During this time, and for the first time, the hotel fell into disrepair.

In 1988 Peter and Camilla Dalglish purchased the Inn and embarked on major renovations three years later. Their dream was to restore the inn to

In the background is the Grafton Village Inn, or Pepper's Tavern as it was known in 1833. The building in the foreground is the local Town Hall.

its former glory. The couple hired Mark Kieffer to begin the renovations, which continued for five years. Mark's objective was to give the building a more open and spacious interior. The main floor was restored to its original design, with the trim and mouldings accurate reproductions of the originals.

It was during these renovations that marvelous discoveries came to light. Old coins, dating from as early as 1814, were found, as well as an assortment of tools. This was when "Fran's" gravestone was discovered in the basement where it was used as a corner foundation support.

A fragment was placed on a windowsill upstairs. It was not long after the renovations were completed that Fran made her presence known.

Lynn Maclean has worked at the Inn for the past three years. Does she believe in ghosts? "I am normally the type of person to have to see before I believe. However, there are things that happen here that you cannot explain, like doors unlocking on their own."

Fran seems to become active at night after the Inn is closed. The problem is that she never locks the

The Grafton Village Inn as it looks today, after renovations.

door upon her return.

Wine glasses that hang above the bar drop and break on their own. Lights go off and on by themselves.

Lynn is not the only employee who believes Fran exists. The chef, Terri Hubbs, adds, "I believe in spirits. There are many things happening here that have no logical explanation. Here at the Inn the doorbell rings whenever someone enters the building. This is part of our security system. Yet you can find the door open during business hours without having heard the bell.

"Our security system would wake the village up if it went off and yet once in awhile you will discover the side door open and no alarm ringing."

It would seem the alarm system is not ghostproof.

Terri has never seen Fran but she has heard her. "I can hear the rustling of a dress on the stairs, yet no one is visible."

The washrooms for the inn are located in the basement. Apparently Fran frequents the Ladies Room. Terri said, "We had to disconnect the electric hand dryer in the women's room. It wouldn't stop running."

When the walk-in fridge was installed, one worker had the fright of his life.

"The man who was installing the compressors felt something or someone touch him on the shoulder. Of course there was no one there," said Terri.

Jackie, the assistant manager, has heard her name called when no was there to call it.

Another employee, Marilyn Popert, has worked at the Inn for the past few years. She has her own share of experiences. Marilyn spends a great deal of time in the basement doing the laundry. She is quite accustomed to Fran's presence there.

"I spend hours in the basement. I don't even realize any more that I am talking aloud to her. The lights often flicker off and on when I am downstairs. Yet, there is such a sense of peace when she's around."

Marilyn recounted the plumber's experiences, "When he was working on the pipes they would begin to rattle at the other end of the building. No one was in that area of the basement at the time."

On another occasion the heat became quite intense from the boiler and no one could adjust the temperature.

"People are very intrigued about the story of Fran. One resident has said we need to convince her that she is lost and needs to be directed on her way," said Marilyn.

It seems this corner of land, this Inn, the cemetery

just behind it, the millpond and this tombstone in the hall window, have a lot of spirit activity. Could any connections be made? Could Fran's full name and history be discovered? There were more questions than answers.

It was time to ask a close friend of mine, another Fran, a well-known Scottish seer, to join me. Fran Harvie is a very gifted person. Her ability to hear and see what others cannot is remarkable. I believe she even has the power to call forth the wind.

We went to the Inn in mid-August. Fran went immediately upstairs to view the tombstone on the window sill. She touched the stone and knew, "Francis Marie was her name. She died in December of 1837. Another individual was buried with her. I am getting the initial G. His name might have been Grant or Graham."

We had some lunch before touring the entire building. As we sat down at the table my attention was drawn to the window. A worker was shovelling earth from a new trench at the back of the old municipal structure next door. I knew the man had made a discovery. He looked shocked and drawn. I excused myself to ask him about it.

"Have you found anything?" I asked.

"Bones", he said.

"Where?"

The man replied, "In the trench, but now they're in that pile of soil."

I was excited, but horrified. Had he actually dug up a grave while Fran and I were looking for ghosts. What a macabre coincidence!

Then he shouted, "Wait a minute. I just found more bones right here in the wall of the trench."

At that moment his boss came around the corner of the building. He asked us what was going on and we showed him the bones and indicated the nearby cemetery. The poor man turned pale. I suggested that he keep all the bones together and notify the proper authorities. With that I returned to the Inn and joined Fran on the tour. Although I was shaken by the discovery of bones, Fran was strangely indifferent.

In the basement Fran moved slowly. "I can sense her presence here. She is very close to the old doorway, which is situated not too far away from where her gravestone was discovered.

"She is not a lost soul. She can't leave even if she wants to! She is bound to the property. She is content to be where she is. There is some connection to a child who was drowned on the property.

"We need to go outside into the backyard. She is leading us."

The ditch beside the Inn in which were found bones on the day our author happened to be there.

We walked toward a grove of lilac near the building. Fran Harvie saw Fran, the ghost, and described her to me because I could see nothing.

"Fran is between 30 and 42 years of age. She has brown hair and is wearing a long dress and jacket. Her dress is grey with shades of lilac or violet trim. She is standing by her grave."

The outline of two gravesites was apparent near my feet. Back in the building Fran said, "Most people expect spirits to be troublesome. This is not necessarily true. Fran's spirit actually enhances this business. She is, after all, watching over her home and loved ones."

A view of the rear of the Grafton Inn. This is where Fran led our author; her grave is near the trees in the foreground.

It seems she is a permanent guest at the Grafton Inn.

The trench turned out to be the final resting place of a cow, which might explain why the discovery of bones didn't elicit a response from Fran Harvie.

If you wish to visit Fran, the lady who stands by her grave, the Grafton Inn will welcome you. Grafton is located on Highway 2 just east of Cobourg, Ontario.

The Bermuda Triangle of the Great Lakes

A place marked by unexplained forces exists out on the open waters of Lake Ontario. Some people refuse to believe it exists. Others light candles and pray.

For the past two hundred years and perhaps more, ships, planes and people have mysteriously vanished into thin air. Unusual objects and lights can be seen there, streaking across the sky. Known to sailors and others as a mysterious place of dread, it was named "The Marysburgh Vortex" in 1980 by Hugh Cochrane in his book, GATEWAY TO OBLIVION.

This account begins in 1883 when the *Quinlan* sailed out of Oswego harbour loaded with coal. She was headed on a course straight through the middle of the Marysburgh Vortex. No one could have foreseen the bizarre events that awaited the ship and crew. Her fate, it seemed, was sealed the

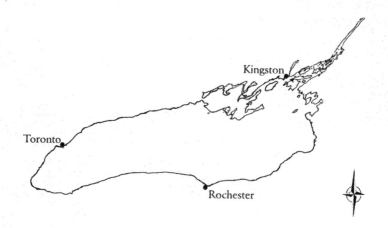

LAKE ONTARIO

moment she was out in open water.

The *Quinlan* sailed into a fog bank. It was greedily engulfed in that misty blanket of moisture. Plummeting temperatures precipitated ice crystals on the deck and railings and snow followed soon after at a driving speed. The crew was unable to keep up with clearing the deck and the churning waters began to swallow the ship and slam its wooden structure. The crew held on for dear life.

The Quinlan was gripped and steered by some unknown force through the Marysburgh Vortex. Witnesses watched from land as her masts were snapped and her hull was split. Eventually she was tossed on the rocks near shore. A few crew-men were rescued, but the others, tangled in rigging or injured, were pulled with the ship back

into the lake, never to be seen again. The few survivors agreed that the ship had been gripped by an
'odd attraction'.

In 1889 the *Armenia*, a tall-masted ship, sailed out
of Kingston harbour at the end of May. The crew
and captain were in search of the mysterious disappearance of another vessel, *Bavaria*.

Nine miles south of the Main Duck Islands the
crew spotted the *Bavaria*, sitting upright on a
small shoal.

As soon as the *Armenia* was within hailing dis-
tance, the crew called out – and were answered by
silence. The solemn mood was broken only by the
creaking of her timbers as the waters of Lake
Ontario nudged her from side to side.

Something was very strange. As the captain and
crew drew alongside, their suspicions were confirmed. The *Bavaria* was a ghost ship. The crew
had completely disappeared without a single trace.
Although a small amount of water was found to be
in her hold, the ship was still seaworthy. A small
repair job, visible on the deck, had been set aside,
as though the seaman had been suddenly interrupted.

What mysterious force had beset the crew of the
Bavaria? Searchers discovered a batch of freshly
baked bread in the galley oven. The captain's
papers were on his desk along with a box contain-
ing a large quantity of money. It had been collected

from cargo recently delivered to American ports. Who would have left the money behind?

In one cabin a canary still chirped in its cage. It was ironic that the only survivor of such a mystery could not tell the tale.

The seamen did discover that one lifeboat was missing. Some men thought an explanation might still be found. The search continued.

On the return of the *Armenia* to Kingston, news of a ghost ship spread throughout the city. People speculated but most importantly the residents began to recall earlier days when others had set sail, never to return. Unnatural happenings out in this region of water on Lake Ontario became the subject of conversation.

Several days later it was reported by the captain of another vessel that there had been a storm at the time. They had sighted a lifeboat with two motionless figures at the oars shortly thereafter but repeated attempts to pull alongside failed. Each time the lifeboat was drawn away. No matter how the captain manoeuvred his vessel, the lifeboat remained out of reach. Eventually, the lifeboat disappeared into a thick fog and was never seen again. The two men in the boat had simply stared blankly and made no effort to be saved.

A lighthouse keeper also reported seeing two men adrift in a boat. He, too, attempted to save the men, but to no avail. According to him, each time he had the boat within his grasp he failed to snag it. He also reported that the men made no sound nor attempt to be saved.

It remains a mystery.

In June of 1900, the ship *Picton*, heavily laden with coal, sailed toward the Marysburgh Vortex. Following in close proximity were the ships *Minnes* and *Acadia*. In a matter of seconds the *Picton* disappeared into thin air. The crews of the *Minnes* and *Acadia* rubbed their eyes in disbelief. Where on earth did the *Picton* go?

While the men prayed silently, the other ships entered the vortex. They searched for hours, yet to no avail. No signs of wreckage, no sign of survivors. They concluded that the *Picton* had somehow vanished into the unknown.

When they reached port on the Canadian side, their crews shared their stories with others. Many listeners nodded their heads as if acknowledging what was already understood: the Marysburgh Vortex was a place where people and ships vanished without trace.

Others hoped for a sign of wreckage or of a lone survivor. A few days later a clue surfaced at Sackets Harbour just a few miles northeast of where the *Picton* was last seen. The young son of a local fishermen spotted a bottle floating in the water just off the harbour. He borrowed his father's boat and rowed out to capture the object. To his amazement he discovered a message from

Captain Sidley in the bottle. Captain Sidley, of the missing *Picton!* The news of such a find became the talk of the district.

What was his message?

Sidley had written that he had lashed himself to his son in order that they could be found together. That was the extent of his hurried note.

Certainly the existence of such a note indicated that the captain and his son did not die suddenly but had experienced some sort of chaos. Some researchers believe the *Picton* entered a doorway to another dimension.

It was the next autumn, 1915, and the end of the shipping season when the *F.C. Barnes* set sail along the north shore of Lake Ontario, headed for Kingston. Witnesses later remarked that while watching the ship from shore it seemed to disappear into a cloud of mist. Once again this occurrence was at the edge of the Marysburgh Vortex.

When the mist dissipated, the tug was no longer visible. Although a search party scoured the waters, no debris was ever found to explain its disappearance. Authorities listed the disappearance of the *F.C Barnes* as "unexplained."

The eeriest story on record is the simple but bizarre story of Captain George Donner. April 28, 1937, Captain Donner and his crew sailed down the middle of Lake Ontario. At 10:15 p.m. the captain ordered the second mate to notify him when they neared their destination and then he retired to his cabin.

A few hours later the second mate knocked at the captain's door. There was no answer. He continued to knock. Something was wrong. He opened the cabin door. No one was there. The crew searched the entire ship. Captain Donner had vanished. Some of the crew testified that they had seen him enter his cabin. Others had heard him moving about in his quarters.

The authorities in port launched a thorough investigation. Nothing turned up. Was it possible that the captain fell overboard? This was quickly discounted since the trip was calm and an experienced sailor like Donner would not have fallen overboard.

Although the authorities alerted all vessels to watch for his body, nothing ever surfaced. Another unsolved mystery.

David Childress, in his book entitled, ANTI-GRAVITY & THE WORLD GRID, described the existence of an earth grid or 'crystalline Earth' in the Marysburgh Vortex.

According to Childress, "This Earth Grid is comprised of geometrical flow lines of gravity in the structure of the Earth itself."

Richard Lefors Clark from San Diego also made reference to this in an article called "Earth Grid,

Human Levitation & Gravity Anomalies." He states, "The pyramids and ley lines are on the power transfer lines of the natural Earth gravity Grid all over the world. The Earth Grid is comprised of the geometrical flow lines of gravity energy in the structure of the Earth itself.

"While the subject of the Earth Grid has been covered in a considerable number of publications, one point in the Grid, marked by a long and strange history at the eastern tip of Lake Ontario is worth special mention."

David Childress also refers to the significant number of aircraft and ship incidents in the Lake Ontario Earth Grid area known as 'The Other Bermuda Triangle' and 'The Gateway to Oblivion' on the eastern end of Lake Ontario.

Clark referred to a project started in 1950 by the Canadian National Research Council and the United States Army to investigate the magnetic anomalies and possible magnetic utility of this area. Officials called it 'Project Magnet'. Was it top secret? Perhaps.

Project Magnet was the first official governmental research program involving the Earth Grid System. Wilbert Smith, a Canadian communications engineer for the Department of Transportation, directed the project. Smith and a team of scientists did find something. However, as Richard Clark explains, "Project Magnet was terminated."

Smith did reveal that there were sometimes mobile gravity anomalies all over the Lake Ontario area. He especially noted areas of 'reduced binding' in the atmosphere above the lake. They described the areas as 'pillar-like columns' a thousand feet up in the atmosphere. Some of these invisible, mysterious columns appear to change location.

One phenomenon that might play a role in the unexplained events here is the number of magnetic anomalies. There are no fewer than fourteen of these magnetic anomalies—areas of strong local magnetic disturbance—plainly marked on present-day navigation charts. The majority of these locations are clustered in the eastern end of Lake Ontario.

In 1804 a very unusual discovery was made in the Marysburgh Vortex. Captain Charles Selleck and his crew of the *Lady Murray* detected something on the surface of the water during a crossing of Lake Ontario. It seemed that in one small area the wave movement was different. The ship was stopped and a lifeboat lowered over the side. He and some crew members rowed to the area to investigate.

What they found was a gigantic stone monolith just three feet (one metre) beneath the surface. It measured forty feet (over 10 metres) square. Sounding it revealed a sheer drop on all sides of approximately 300 feet (less than 100 metres) straight down.

The captain entered his findings in his logbook;

this object was a major navigation hazard and others needed that knowledge. Curious seekers sailed out to poke and prod this immense monolith for some months to follow. Among the visitors to the site was Captain Thomas Paxton of the government schooner *Speedy*. No one knew what this foreshadowed for Captain Paxton. An event near the village of Port Perry on Lake Scugog would precipitate the experience.

In 1806 the Farewell family opened a trading post for barter with the Native peoples on Washburn's Island on Lake Scugog. One day the Farewells left their agent, John Sharp, in charge of the post. When they returned, they found him dead. It was alleged that a Native named Ogetonicut had done the deed to avenge the murder, by a white man, of his brother, Whistling Duck. Ogetonicut was arrested and after a preliminary hearing it was decided that the trial would be held at the Newcastle courthouse.

Newcastle was the new district town planned for Northumberland and Durham to be located at Presqui'le. The murder had been committed in that judicial district. Ogetonicut was taken first to York, now Toronto, to await transportation to Presqui'le. A government schooner named the *Speedy* was chartered in October to take those who needed to be present at the trial down the lake. Judge Thomas Cochrane, court officials, and a selected group of dignitaries were to officiate.
The *Speedy* had two alternate captains. One was Thomas Paxton and the other was James

Richardson. Apparently Richardson had some fore-warning concerning the trip, his intuition told him not to go. There was danger. He attempted to change the minds of the officials. Even the witnesses refused to board. Paxton, however, was ordered to do the job.

According to local lore, Ogetonicut's mother travelled from Lake Scugog to the shores of Lake Ontario near Oshawa to watch for the *Speedy* to go by. When she caught sight of the vessel, and in the knowledge that her son was on board, she began to chant against those who had taken him away.

That evening a violent storm struck. By midnight, enormous waves crashed the shore. The *Speedy* was being pursued by a deadly gale. Captain Paxton, for some unknown reason, never sought the shelter of the harbours he passed in the night. Instead, the ship steered straight for Presqu'ile Bay.

As the ship neared its destination, locals lit bonfires to help direct the ship into harbour, but the *Speedy* seemed to be on a different course. Hugh Cochrane elaborates, "The captain paid them no heed. Nor did he appear to have control of his vessel, for her course seemed unerring. As if drawn by a huge magnet, the ship headed directly for the area of the monolith, then was lost from sight as the storm closed over the scene."

That was the last time anyone saw the *Speedy*.

The ship had simply disappeared. The next day searchers sailed out to the area of the monolith hoping to find either survivors or wreckage of the ship. They were shocked when they dragged the lake and found nothing. Even the stone monolith was gone. There was no longer a three hundred foot depth of water, instead it was shallow and sandy.

No wreckage and no survivors of the *Speedy* were ever found.

Janet Kellough is a 7th generation Prince Edward County resident. She knows about the existence of the Marysburgh Vortex. "When you're in a recreational boat your compass doesn't work out there. I know a pilot who was flying out over the middle of the vortex when he encountered a strange phenomena. It was like a giant hand reached out and flipped his plane over. Then a sudden force uprighted the craft. People also report seeing strange lights out over these waters."

Dave Whatton has lived in Prince Edward County for the past fifty-four years. He is a local historian who is most knowledgeable concerning these events and theories about this mysterious area in Ontario. I asked David a number of pertinent questions about the Marysburgh Vortex.

"I will say that many of the doomed sailors on the vessels that disappeared undoubtedly experienced some form of shock, which has certain effects as to separate various aspects of the Etheric body from the other layers. This results in emotionally charged fragments that loop. We know them as 'ghosts.' They are quite akin to an endless loop video of a few seconds duration. The figure appears, does its thing, then disappears, only to repeat the scene any number of times.

"This repeating pattern has been noted throughout the world, and certainly has manifested itself in this area. I recognize that the phenomenon is truly real to the perceiver and that certain individuals are more able to receive this sensory-based communication than others.

"I live in the so-called Marysburgh Vortex. It is a quiet, rural area populated by a mixture of classic farm and fisher folk plus city escapists.

"The specific area referred to by some as the Marysburgh Vortex is in the extreme southeastern sector of Prince Edward County, bounded by water on three sides with no more than two miles of land separating an arm of inland sea, namely Prince Edward Bay from Lake Ontario proper.

"The Marysburgh Vortex is more than just a mysterious place where people, boats and planes go missing, it is a sacred territory emitting a strong atmosphere of mysticism and healing qualities.

As to the spirituality of the area, David points out that shamans of various native cultures spanning thousands of years have treated this area as sacred. The Hopewell/Adena (circa 300 BC) not only settled in this spot for several hundred years but built their Mounds here as well. "Two thousand years later, the island of Waupoos was named after a Cayuga holy man. The ancients knew that this area was special and I concur."

If you plan to sail in The Marysburgh Vortex or even pay a visit, keep your eyes peeled for the unusual—lights, mists and vanishing objects. Keep your ears keened and listening for unexplained cries in the night and keep your mind and other senses tuned and open. The mystery continues.

3

Marilyn at French River

Ayoung woman disembarks at the train station. Her black hair is covered by a scarf and she is wearing big, dark glasses. She hunches over slightly as she walks. No one would guess her real identity. The owner of the local lodge, Clarence Honey, however, recognises her.

"Hello, Miss Munroe. So nice to see you again. Please step this way and I'll get your bags."

Marilyn Monroe was accustomed to travelling incognito and sometimes used the name 'Zelda Zonk' when she did. Zelda was only one of the aliases she used. She also wore a black wig and, sometimes, old baggy clothing. She had learned early that she had to be more than one person.

And who was she really? Was she a Proust-reading sex kitten or was she a frightened child, caught up in the unforgiving world of the movies?

People who knew Marilyn well claimed she could turn on her 'Marilyn persona' at will. She could appear in public unnoticed and suddenly lift her head, straighten her posture, flash her smile, toss her hair—and become the glorious Marilyn Monroe.

Shelly Winters, who shared an apartment with Marilyn early in her career, said, "She'd come out of our apartment in a shleppy old coat, looking like my maid, and all the people would push her aside to get *my* autograph. She loved it."

It proved to be hard work, turning this persona on and off and it must have been even harder knowing when to flip the switch.

The late, great director, Billy Wilder, directed Marilyn twice, in *The Seven Year Itch* when her marriage to Joe DiMaggio fell apart and in *Some Like It Hot* when she and Arthur Miller were having marital problems.

Wilder was famously quoted as saying "Her marriages didn't work out because Joe DiMaggio found out she was Marilyn Monroe, and Arthur Miller found out she *wasn't* Marilyn Monroe."

He also said, "One side of Marilyn was wonderful, and the other side was terrible. She was two of a kind."

Marilyn was a Gemini and called herself, "Jekyll and Hyde. Two in one." She said, "I think when you are famous every weakness is exaggerated."

How heart-breaking it must have been to know
that you must always, ultimately, disappoint those
you love, including, of course, your legions of fans.
And love her they did, although during her lifetime
it was often a guilty pleasure. Marilyn was largely
either a figure of lust or scorn.

In the 1950's Marilyn Monroe was considered
shocking. She was a sensation and everything she
did or wore created huge interest. Church officials
advised their congregations not to see her movies,
even though the clothing she wore in them was
carefully censored: her shorts must not be too
short, her dresses not cut too low.

Joan Crawford openly criticized her wardrobe and
called her a tart. The press delighted in describing
her walk: Did she exaggerate the swing of her hips
by trimming the heel of only one shoe? Had one
hip been dislocated?

Through it all, Marilyn *appeared* innocent and
slightly oblivious, as if she couldn't quite compre-
hend what all the fuss was about. Pauline Kael
explained this facade by calling her a 'baby whore'.

"I learned to walk early and I've been doing it ever
since," or "What do I have on when I go to bed?
Why, the radio, of course."

Billy Wilder perfectly captured this attitude in his

movies, especially *The Seven Year Itch*, where Marilyn plays a 22-year-old actress, puzzled at why men keep falling for her. Both movies Billy Wilder made with Marilyn stand the test of time and deserve a look today.

That was the screen Marilyn. The real Marilyn, however, had to make a life for herself, somehow away from the image that had been created.

Allan 'Whitey' Snyder, Marilyn's devoted make-up man said, "She had the greatest inferiority complex of any person I ever knew."

He also said "She's fightened to death of the public who think she is so sexy. My God, if they only knew how hard it is for her."

Marilyn Monroe made two movies in Canada. *Niagara*, with Joseph Cotton and Jean Peters, was filmed in Niagara Falls, Ontario and New York in the summer of 1952 and was released in January, 1953.

River of No Return, with Robert Mitchum and Rory Calhoun, was filmed in Jasper National Park in Alberta in the summer of 1953 and released in 1954. She was no stranger to the Canadian north and spent considerable time there.

Late in 1954 she endured a hospital stay and, as the press of the time recorded eagerly, openly broke down as she was being discharged. In December she split with Joe DiMaggio. 1955 was to be the start of a new life for her.

In January she formed her own company with the photographer Milton Greene. She was one of the first movie stars to try to control her own career. She said at the time that she was going to change her whole life and the public's attitude to her by acting in important plays and writing poetry.

Marilyn Monroe wanted to be taken seriously, she knew what we came to know later: she was a gifted actress and talented comedienne.

Yet, in June of that year *The Seven Year Itch* premiered, with images of a flirtatious, bubble-headed Marilyn, her skirt billowing over her shoulders. That scene, incidently, also marked the end of the marriage to Joe DiMaggio.

Between June and December of 1955, when she signed a contract with Twentieth-Century-Fox, she was not filming and desperately needed time off. She escaped to Ontario in the fall.

Her partner in Marilyn Monroe Productions, Milton Greene, hired a young man to act as her driver and escort. The late Jack Jensen, who went on to become a well-known member of the book publishing community, became very close to Ms Monroe during this period.

We can't confirm she visited French River late in 1955 but she certainly had the time and opportunity to do so then.

She also may have visited a retreat in the fall of 1957. This would have occurred after yet another

Jack Jensen, hired by Milton Greene, in late 1955 with Marilyn Monroe. Mr. Jensen was her driver and escort while she visited Ontario.

particularly turbulent time in her life when her husband of just one year, Arthur Miller, had to endure a protracted court battle. Marilyn stood by him and, of course, attracted more attention to the case.

She was in New York City in July and miscarried a pregnancy on August 4. It would have been wise to escape and recuperate at such a point. Again, she may have visited French River to recover.

People in French River who remember Marilyn recall a visit in the summer of 1958.

This would be consistent with her wish to get healthy for, on July 8, she arrived in New York City from California and happily confessed to the await-ing press that she was 'overweight.' On August 28, she announced her pregnancy. She and her hus-band, Arthur Miller, were jubilant at the prospect of a baby.

Shortly after the announcement she was on the set of *Some Like it Hot* for nine weeks. Her costars and the director of this film have said she was in terri-ble shape emotionally. During the shoot, she had to be hospitalized for 'nerves' at one point. She then returned to New York City on November 23 and on December 16 the news of her miscarriage became public.

Marilyn's mental state worsened throughout the new year and in June, 1959, she had another medical procedure which she hoped would prevent future miscarriages.

She stayed out of the public eye until that fall, during which time she would have had the opportunity to go north to the French River again.

By 1960, Marilyn found herself in a complex relationship with Yves Montand, the late French movie star. He and his wife, the late Simone Signoret (who, ironically, had just won an Oscar for her role as an abandoned, suicidal mistress in *A Room at the Top*) became great friends with Marilyn and Arthur Miller.

They had adjacent bungalows at the Beverly Hills Hotel and dined together every night during the shooting of *Let's Make Love*, the movie Marilyn made with Mr. Montand.

Alas, the lives of celebrities are never their own—Marilyn's life was a perfect example—and separations are unavoidable. Ms Signoret and Mr. Miller had commitments elsewhere and Marilyn and Yves Montand were left alone together.

Their love affair was a disaster for Marilyn. When Yves Montand returned to Europe he said, "If Marilyn hadn't been such a baby, there wouldn't have been so much gossip."

Simone Signoret, of course, was no longer close to Marilyn although she had the intellect and understanding to give this affair the importance it deserved. In her wonderful book, *NOSTALGIA ISN'T WHAT IT USED TO BE,* she wrote lovingly of her relationship with Marilyn and said she treasured a scarf Marilyn gave her. Although it was frayed at one edge, she simply turned that edge in to hide the flaw, undoubtedly a metaphor for a flaw in Marilyn that Ms Signoret chose to forgive.

Marilyn's reaction to the end of the affair was not as sanguine. In June she overdosed on sleeping pills. In July she travelled to Nevada to begin filming *The Misfits*, written for her by her husband, and she arrived dishevelled and ungroomed. The press had a field day describing her confused and weary condition.

In August she overdosed again on barbiturates. She was hospitalized and when filming ended in the fall, she and Arthur Miller separated.

Shortly after shooting ended Clark Gable, her co-star and father figure, died and there were accusations that Marilyn's behaviour on the set had precipitated his fatal heart attack. Not surprisingly, Marilyn's mental state deteriorated disturbingly.

The following February she was hospitalized again, and would be in and out of clinics and hospitals during 1961, as she was in and out of liaisons with John F. Kennedy, Frank Sinatra and her former husband, Joe DiMaggio.

She learned that another ex-husband, Arthur Miller, had married the talented Inge Morath, a photographer who was on the set of *The Misfits*.

It was some time during late 1960 or early 1961

that Marilyn began ingesting more powerful drugs and she travelled to Mexico in early 1962 where she acquired even more of them.

As far as the press was concerned, it was now 'open season' on Marilyn. As her public behaviour became more bizarre and she was often obviously high or drunk or distressed by the media frenzy around her, the press became more aggressive. Marilyn Monroe's traumas were big news and sold newspapers and magazines and, of course, no matter how ill she became, she was always beautifully photogenic.

In March, 1962, she was awarded the Golden Globe Award for her performance in *The Misfits*. The televised event did not include her acceptance as she was obviously incapacitated. Photos that appeared in the press show a droopy-eyed, vacuous beauty, kissing her wine glass or slumped against Rock Hudson who presented her award.

By April she was shooting *Something's Got to Give* at the ailing 20th Century Fox studios. She took a break in May to make her famous appearance at John F. Kennedy's party at Madison Square Gardens to sing 'Happy Birthday, Mr. President', a very public declaration of their romantic involvement. In all photos of that event, a discreet First Lady, Jacqueline Kennedy, is not to be seen. She apparently excused herself and returned when Marilyn departed.

Marilyn's illnesses stopped the shooting of *Something's Got to Give*—the only film being shot on the studio lot since the excesses of *Cleopatra* left the studio financially strapped. In June the studio fired her. This put people out of work and she was publicly blamed.

On August 5, 1961, the news of her death was reported. Conspiracy theories were rife and they still surface, however, her death was declared a suicide and was probably accidental.

Marilyn had admitted to her friends that she had tried to commit suicide several times and said that suicide was, "a person's privilege. I don't believe it's a sin or a crime. It's your right if you want to, 'though it doesn't get you anywhere."

The French River Resort in the 1940's

Yesterdays' main lodge as it is today

Arthur Miller said, "Beneath all her insouciance and wit, death was her companion everywhere and at all times, and it may be that its acknowledged presence was what lent her poignancy, dancing at the edge of oblivion as she was."

Whitey Snyder made her up for the last time for her funeral. He had promised he would, in jest, and she reminded him with a money clip engraved: "Whitey Dear, While I'm still warm, Marilyn."

There were many periods during her very stressful existence that she could have, and should have, gone to French River. Certainly the quiet surroundings, fresh air and good, wholesome food would be a far cry from the life she led in

Chalet 15
An idyllic getaway spot. Is she still in residence?

Hollywood. We know more than once in the 1950s this troubled, anxious and frail young woman sought sanctuary at the Chalet Bungalow Lodge.

She didn't need to be a star on the French River. She wasn't hounded by press agents or fans. The people at the inn respected her privacy and understood her need for solitude. Why wouldn't she want to stay there forever?

The staff certainly think she has.

*   *   *   *

In 1923 Canadian Pacific Railway officials were looking for ways to increase passenger service on the line from Toronto to Sudbury. An elite tourist fishing resort was built on the French river at the

French River Train Station brought visitors from all over the world to the quiet Canadian north.

hub of a maze of waterways, looking west toward the Recollet Falls. It was only 200 yards (80 metres) from the train station and offered self-contained suites, described in the company's brochure as:

> "...a cluster of charming rustic bungalows ... simple but abundantly comfortable, having ... running water, electric light, and a spacious verandah ... the rates at French River Bungalow Camp are $5.00 per day, $30.00 per week, American plan. ...a fast train leaves Toronto in the morning, giving connections from New York, Buffalo, Pittsburgh and Cleveland."

One of the breathtaking vistas at Yesterdays

Bungalow Camp enjoyed many famous visitors over the years. In 1939 during the Royal Tour before World War II, King George VI and Queen Elizabeth enjoyed dinner in the main dining room and stayed in their private rail car on the property. In honour of this visit, the stonework in the dining room's fireplace was arranged in the shape of the King's crown. This feature is still intact.

A view from the main lodge in winter.

In 1945 the property was sold to Clarence E. Honey who operated it successfully until 1965. During the 1950's the camp gained a reputation as a retreat for several Hollywood celebrities. Clark Gable and Ray Bolger, known best for his role as the scarecrow in the *Wizard of Oz,* signed the guest register.

Marilyn Monroe, too, discovered Bungalow Camp and stayed in chalet 15. Locals there remember that she enjoyed the simple, rustic life but she seemed nervous and on the verge of hysteria. She needed the peace this place could help to give her. Many of the workers at the lodge believe it has held her there.

Since 1965 the resort has changed hands several times and has been renamed. It was in 1992 that the place was named Yesterdays, a very appropriate name as the past does tend to linger there. There is a strange, quiet and timeless feel to the place. The guests of the past seem to mingle with the guests of the present.

Larry and Janis Pichette now own and operate the resort which features 22 chalets, a spacious dining room that can accommodate up to 150 diners, a spa, tennis courts, recreation centre and conference room. Janis is not shy about admitting the presence of unseen guests. She has had several experiences since 1995. Does she believe Marilyn Monroe is still there?

"I have heard it from too many people that she is

really here. Guests see a beautiful blonde woman who appears and then immediately disappears. One Sunday night in the winter when we were closed I was all alone working in the office. Suddenly the door opened by itself. You could feel someone was there. Then I saw her. A vaporous form."

You may sit by the fire and hear music coming from some invisible source. Doors open as though someone is entering the main lodge. On occasion the coffee pot is emptied by some unseen visitor.

Andrea Lehman, a young housekeeper at the lodge, believes a spirit inhabits chalet 15. "When I am working in #15, I can feel someone there with me, but no one ever appears to me. The person is over in the corner of the room."

Sandy Rancourt, another employee, told me about a couple who had been married at the lodge in 1946 and came back to celebrate their 50th wedding anniversary. "They stayed in chalet 15. The couple saw the apparition of a beautiful blonde woman who appeared in front of them."

In that chalet, coffee stir sticks keep appearing on the floor. Staff keep replacing them on the appropriate shelf but when they return, the sticks are again on the floor. They all believe Marilyn inhabits the lodge.

Sandy MacKean is the executive chef at the resort. He feels he is never alone in the kitchen and gave me several examples of why he feels that way. "The coffeemaker will start on its own. You ll make a pot of coffee and then come back and discover that someone has drunk three-quarters of the pot. Marilyn especially loved coffee; it was her favourite drink, after *Dom P rignon* champagne.

The door by the kitchen wait station will swing wide open and then shut on its own. I have even seen a shadow go by. I thought it was one of the staff, until I realized I was all alone. I tried to turn the stove on and it was already going. I have heard the walk-in fridge door open and close. Utensils and pots rattle in the kitchen when no one is there.

The staff working in the dining room often see a shadow following behind them. It is not unusual to find the silverware rearranged on the tables. Both Pam Couvrette and Nathalie Joncas, two of the staff, have heard their names called several times, by a woman.

The bar at Yesterdays. The glasses sometimes rattle at the cocktail hour.

Nathalie told me "Sometimes I will be sitting by the fireplace and I will hear a woman singing."

I sat in a wing chair in the lobby at 5:00 p.m. when glasses hanging over the bar in the lobby area began to rattle against one another. All the staff agree that there is more paranormal activity late in the day and at night.

The week following my visit with Janis and the staff, the activity increased significantly. The abundance of paranormal activity included an apparition in the dining room, the kitchen door to the outside opened and closed on its own, the telephone system went crazy and the cash register decided to tally its own figures. There has never been so much activity during such a short time.

It's certain Marilyn hasn't stayed in Hollywood. She once said, " Hollywood is a place where they'll pay you a thousand dollars for a kiss and fifty cents for your soul. I know, because I turned down the first offer often enough and held out for the fifty cents."

Yesterdays really is aptly named; you can step out of time there. Your chance of having an experience with a guest of the past is highly probable; one of them may be the restless spirit of Marilyn Monroe.

Emma's Back Porch

A figure in a black, lace-topped evening dress devotes her attention to the arrival and departure of her guests. She is the *grande dame* of the Estaminet Restaurant in Burlington and has been since 1919 when Emma and George Byrens purchased an old house that looked out over Lake Ontario on Water Street, now Lakeshore Road. Emma's dream was to open a grand dining establishment and she started with just four tables.

Emma had good taste. She purchased food locally and insisted on the best. When the restaurant was closed, she busied herself in the kitchen preparing preserves for sale. Word of mouth spread and her restaurant was a success.

Over the years the Estaminet grew in size and reputation. It was 'the place' to be seen and to dine. The inscription written in Emma's first guest book testifies to her outlook on life and on business. "A

Mrs. Emma Byrens, proud proprietor of the Estaminet Restaurant, now called Emma's Back Porch

The original Estaminet Restaurant

human document rich in contemporary history; a record of the most pleasant side of our times." Later guest books are filled with the signatures of dignitaries, politicians, entertainers and socialites from all around the world. These visitors included Liberace, Louis Armstrong, Prime Minister John Diefenbaker, Prime Minister Lester B. Pearson, and Barbara Ann Scott.

One Mothers' Day, Ontario Premier Mitchell F. Hepburn, with Mrs. Hepburn and a party of friends, dined there. In May 1931, Viscount Duncannon, son of Canada's new Governor-General, Lord Bessborough, had dinner with a group of friends. After the meal, the Viscount personally congratulated Mrs. Byrens on her excellent establishment.

Emma contributed greatly to the Second World War effort. On one occasion she organized a card party for 400 guests with the proceeds going to the Burlington district branch of the Canadian Red Cross. In 1943, on her 70th birthday, a gala event was held at the Estaminet to celebrate her life.

Emma was not yet ready to throw in the towel, however. She continued as proprietess until she retired in 1952 – and perhaps she has remained even longer.

The Estaminet changed hands several times until 1992. At that time Kalin Johnson and Craig Kowalchuk took over and it was renamed 'Emma's Back Porch'. It still really does belong to Emma.

Kalin and Craig had a great sense about the history of this site. The area downstairs was turned into a roadhouse bar and lounge, a cozy cottage-like room with a fireplace. They created an elegant semi-formal setting called The Water Street Cookery where they feature mouth-watering pasta and seafood dishes.

The existence of Emma's spirit was news to Kalin and Craig. They delighted to take it as an omen of prosperity. Emma obviously approves of the new arrangements since she graces the restaurant by standing at one of the windows or walking about the premises.

She has been seen many times. Patrons have been tapped on the shoulder or literally have had their menus pulled out of their hands by some unseen force.

When they began renovations in the early 1990s, workers heard screaming when the ceiling was removed. The renovations eliminated part of the living quarters on the second floor where Emma, her husband and her family once resided.

Three original and magnificent stained-glass windows, once visible from the exterior, are now part of the lobby décor. An English 16-foot grandfather clock stands in the entrance. A sweeping staircase to the second floor is decorated with many historic photographs and framed pages of Emma's guest books.

A psychic session was held in the building a few years ago and resulted in communication with Emma. Craig said "I knew I was here to take care of her building, and that she would be a good ghost to me after that session."

Kelly Lawlor is the manager of Emma's Back Porch. She does not believe in paranormal activity, but admits to feeling a chill now and then. She does also concede that her staff have had many unexplained experiences in the place.

"Emma is mainly seen upstairs in The Water St. Cookery. Staff have seen her walk by the windows of the dining lounge. Customers sitting outside on the lakeside deck have seen Emma gazing out the second storey windows towards the lake. Most staff members prefer not to venture upstairs after closing time.

"Emma often appears with her white hair in a bun and she is dressed in a black blouse and skirt. One night at 1:30 a.m. a staff member saw her walking around downstairs."

Kelly also feels another spirit exists in the building, that of Emma's son, who apparently drowned at a young age in the lake behind the Estaminet. Perhaps we are witnessing a bizarre reunion.

Some of the staff have been there since Kalin and Craig took over. In the early 1990s the beer fridge was upstairs in The Water St. Cookery. On one occasion a waitress went upstairs for some beer. When she opened the fridge door, much to her surprise, the ghost of a little boy was standing inside, crying. She fled. That same waitress still has a problem with the beer fridge.

"Today we keep the beer in a fridge located in the basement. I have to use all my strength to open and close the fridge door. Two male employees say they have opened the door to have it close on its own."

Another waitress spoke of an experience that happened several years ago. A co-worker caught sight of a dark shadow that moved across the downstairs room at about 2:30 a.m. and left quickly via the front door.

Journalist Carmela Fragomeni of *The Hamilton Spectator*, wrote about Emma's Back Porch. "Both Johnson and Kowalchuck talked of their own unusual experiences, and those they heard from their employees, of books flying off the shelves and a large hand-operated salad spinner on the kitchen floor spinning like crazy on its own for about five minutes without decelerating."

Laurel Haber, a long-time resident of Burlington, recalls Emma. "My father's first wife was Emma's niece. Emma did a lot of charity work for the town of Burlington. She really cared about the poor.

"Sunday was the big family day. When you arrived at the Estaminet you entered the front doors and

Emma's original dining room.

proceeded to a waiting room off to the right called the anteroom. Emma would be there, standing behind a lectern. She was the *grande dame*. She always wore a black evening dress and a silver chain around her neck.

"You would be led down the hall to a huge expansive dining room. I can still recall the décor. There were Chinese lanterns with large red silk tassels hanging from the ceiling. The waiters were dressed in black trousers and white shirts. The waitresses wore French maid outfits. The water was poured from a silver pitcher. This place was Emma's baby. She was welcoming you into her home."

There are indications that two of Emma's children have remained behind. Her young son, who drowned, has not only been seen in the upstairs fridge, but also in the basement. Emma had a daughter who also died unexpectedly. She has been heard from in the basement.

This basement is a very eerie place. There are two secret tunnels from the cellar area. They are covered over now, but one tunnel ran under the street to a house and the second tunnel faced the lake. There are no accounts of these tunnels but some historians think they may have been constructed for use during prohibition days, since Burlington and the Hamilton Bay were very active in the rum-running trade. It could also have connected with the 'underground railroad'. Neither of these events, however, could have involved Emma because the days of the 'railroad' were before her time and because she did not sell illegal liquor during prohibition.

On Halloween of 2001, a ghost investigation was conducted by Canadian ghost expert Patrick Cross and paranormal investigator Carolyn Bassell. (Patrick has been hired by real estate brokers to get rid of unwanted ghosts.) He found the ghost of Emma's husband and also discovered the spirits of five happy children playing in the basement. He even managed to photograph the shadowy figures of what appear to be Emma, her husband, George, and one child in the cellar area.

Carolyn recalls the first visit to Emma's. "We went to the basement. We picked up a number of spirits there. We heard laughter. I received the name Simon or Steven. The children appear happy and are quite mischievous. There is also the spirit of a man lurking near the tunnel entrances.

"We discovered a cold spot in the kitchen area. Everyone felt quite dizzy. I felt like I was being pulled down. It was here where I contacted a male spirit who had suffered a heart attack. It is quite possible he died here. I was able to send him on his way."

Carolyn was also able to locate Emma in the restaurant. "I picked up the spirit of Emma on the first floor in the log-cabin room. She was sitting on a bench near the stone fireplace. She was wearing a lace-collared, grey dress.

"I noticed some spirit energy near the staircase

leading up to The Water Street Cookery. I also located a spirit in the upstairs dining lounge, near the seating area. I felt that this spirit had had a long illness and possibly died here."

In December of 2001, Carolyn returned once again. "This time I was just outside the kitchen entrance door. There was a gate in the laneway. As soon as I started walking, the gate began to swing back and forth on its own."

There does seem to be a variety of spirit activity at Emma's. It seems that Emma, in fact, has not retired from the business. Perhaps your dining experience would be the better for your acknowledgement of Emma, the *grande dame*, when you place your order.

5

Everything Happens in Room #4

The historic village of Bayfield, perched above the sandy shoreline of Lake Huron, has a long, strong past. Civic pride is a tradition and the folks in Bayfield are very friendly. During our visit there we had one of the warmest welcomes my wife and I have ever had anywhere. Especially at the Albion Hotel.

The Albion Hotel is located on the main street and it feels just like home. The staff are courteous and welcoming. The structure was built in the 1840's and was designed to be a store. The proprietor, Robert Reid, built an addition in 1856 and the Albion opened its doors as a hotel. Since that time the hotel has catered to the needs of villagers and tourists.

In 1897 it was the scene of a murder.

The village of Bayfield got its start as a port. Rich

The shores of Lake Huron

agricultural land to the east produced valued crops for shipping and fishing had a lot to offer. Lake Huron is beautiful to start with and here was a spot with a natural harbour and a rivermouth, an ideal location for settlement. The land upon which the village was founded was originally purchased, sight unseen, by Baron van Tuyll van Serooskerten of Hague. He had been advised to do so by his good friend Admiral Henry Bayfield, who had served as a surveyor on the Great Lakes. The settlement took the Admiral's name.

Bayfield was laid out on a radial plan with a town

The original Albion Hotel, Bayfield.

square at the hub of the wheel. The main street is situated at the north west corner of one of the spokes. By the 1850's that main street was a hub of activity with many shops and industry. There were half a dozen hotels operating throughout the village and there was an air of abundance.

Unfortunately, it was not to last because of choices made by the railway. The new line by-passed Bayfield and was built at Goderich, just a few miles up the Lake Huron shore. Industry withered and died.

The locals were a resourceful lot and soon this picturesque village began to recover. Perhaps the railway did them a favour because, instead of industry, they got tourists and an abundance of lovely summer homes.

The local newspaper in 1895 attested to this, "A few years ago Bayfield was little heard of outside the country; today she is talked of and widely famed as a pleasant and beautiful watering place."

Tourists fell in love with the quaint atmosphere of the village and its beautiful landscape. The trees there are magnificent; even today there is a slippery elm reported to be 560 years old.

Although serene on the surface, as in any community there were secrets, distrust, alcohol abuse and, in this town, even murder. Murder can create a situation in which one or more souls become trapped at the scene of the crime. This, no doubt, explains one aspect of the paranormal activity occurring at the Albion Hotel.

In the 1890's Maria and Edward Elliott were the proprietors of the Albion and it was also their home. The Elliotts had much sorrow in their family. By 1895 they had already buried three sons, the youngest was only 14 years old and the eldest was 28.

Maria, her daughter Lily, and her two sons, Fred and Harvey, shared the daily chores at the hotel. It was well known that Harvey had an argumentative nature and became worse when he drank.

On a Monday in November of 1897, 21 year-old Harvey and his friend, Dumart, went out drinking in nearby Varna, a village located four miles (6.4 kms.)

from Bayfield.

About 8:30 p.m. Harvey and Dumart returned home to the Albion. It didn't take too long for Harvey to have yet another drink in the bar, what is today the dining room, and then to quarrel with his 19 year-old brother, Fred. There was trouble brewing. The boys left the bar.

Fred was standing outside the hall door. Harvey was standing on the platform in front of the hotel. Then he shouted to Fred, "Go into the house."

George Erwin, a witness to the events, stated that he heard Harvey swearing at his brother. Harvey was in a temper as Erwin and his sister Lily tried to restrain him from striking his brother. Lily screamed for help.

The family knew that the brothers were not in the habit of quarrelling except when Harvey had been drinking. Mrs. Elliot rushed to Fred to talk to him. Harvey was only a few feet away when someone caught sight of a revolver in Fred's hand. Fred then shouted, "Keep him away from me or I'll shoot him."

Suddenly Harvey broke away and pulled off his coat. Standing there he yelled, "Here's somebody who is not afraid of being shot."

Then Harvey charged Fred; Fred raised the gun and it went off. Harvey fell into his friend's arms. The bullet had passed through his trachea.

Fred stood still for a moment and then tears welled

Entance foyer of the Albion Hotel where Harvey Elliot was shot.

up in his eyes. He had shot his own brother. Although missing from the newspaper accounts, it was rumoured that they tried to get Harvey to the water pump for a drink before they took him inside.

Harvey was, eventually carried into the bar, where he died within seconds. His blood permanently stained the wooden floor.

Fred was tried for murder. The locals took up a petition for clemency but the jury returned a tough verdict: "Guilty; with a strong recommendation to mercy."

The judge sentenced Fred to several years in the Kingston Penitentiary. He was released early due to

The Albion Hotel today.

poor health. He died on September 13, 1905 at the age of 28.

As for Harvey, it seems he has remained at the place of his death.

Although there have been no visual sightings to confirm the identity, someone likes to turn a light on at night in the bar area after the hotel has closed for the night. Someone likes to flip a beer tap on occasion, too. Psychics have confirmed a male presence in the new dining area.

Kim Muszynski talks about the Albion. Upon his return from the west where he had worked for Delta Western, he went out with his family for lunch at the Albion Hotel in Bayfield. Today he owns it.

"I never heard any stories of spirits or hauntings until we began some renovation work downstairs."

The renovations involved moving the original bar from the left side, as you enter, to the right side. Kim then turned the old bar area into an old-fashioned dining room furnished with simple antiques.

The present-day bar is a very friendly place. Copper-topped tables of all sizes and miscellaneous chairs furnish the area. A gas fireplace is both warm and atmospheric. In former years this room was a gathering-place and had held a player piano.

It was during these renovations that Kim encountered his first indication of paranormal activity. "We finished the work downstairs and were just getting started upstairs.

"I had hired a painter who said that he didn't paint unless there was music playing. So we provided him with a portable stereo. We had all just started working when the radio went off on its own. This happened three times for no apparent reason."

Kim was not convinced the hotel was haunted—but that soon changed. "One night my partner, John, who was sleeping in the next room upstairs in the hotel came into my room twice. He heard his name being called. He thought I had called him, but I hadn't.

The Albion Bar yesterday and today.

"Then, on the second occasion, just when I was about to drift off to sleep, I felt a hand touch my face. I didn't sleep for the rest of the night."

Nancy was a young woman who married a local farmer by the name of John. The odd thing was that she never went to live with her husband. Instead, she lived at the Albion Hotel in the room that Kim had used as a bedroom and which is now the common room. Her husband visited the hotel to be with her.

Nancy lived there until she died. Perhaps she still calls his name in the night.

There has been activity over the years, particularly during any renovations, but it had been quiet in the last few months. That is, until I made an appointment for an interview.

The night before I arrived Kim had a very unusual experience at his home. "I have two dogs. When I went to feed them I took a cup of dog food and filled the first dish, then I got a cup for the other one and put that in the dish. What the...the cup was full of water! Where did that water come from? I checked the dogs' pail and it was full of water. It wasn't possible for any water to get in there. I thought it was a prank or something.

"Then at 9 a.m. the next morning I was at the hotel sitting in the pub reading your book, HAUNTED ONTARIO, and occasionally glancing up to watch the Olympics on the television. A guest staying in

The second floor at the Albion Hotel is a very busy area for ghosts.

Room 4 came down and inquired if the bar television was connected to the television in his room. I said it wasn't. It's all cable. He said that he was watching CNN when someone or something changed the channels."

When my wife and I arrived at the Albion we were warmly greeted by Kim, Shelly Know, the hotel manager, Jack (Kim's dad), and Stella and Betty, Jack's friends. Jack informed me that Betty was sensitive to spirit activity and wanted to join in the investigation.

This light in the dining room turns itself on at night.

The tour of the hotel began in the dining room which was originally the bar and where Harvey Elliott had died. Kim said the gun Fred used to kill his brother was found behind the bar.

Betty said, "I feel three spots in this room that give me the chills. I have goosebumps on my arms. The presence is male."

Upstairs there are seven bedsitting rooms. Kim led us into the common room, which had been Kim's bedroom. Shelly Know, who has managed the hotel for the past several years, spoke about the unexplained activity in the building.

"Not many years ago we were hosting the annual golf tournament. We were sitting in this common room folding t-shirts when four books suddenly flew off the bookcase. The employee with me fled downstairs."

Shelly placed the books back on the shelf and went back to the pub. She returned later to discover the same books back on the floor again.

"Another day, after closing, we were sitting here in the common room when we heard the door at the top of the stairs open and close. We were the only ones in the building. Then we heard footsteps."

One night Shelly and three other employees got the shock of their lives in the pub area. "It was midnight and we were closed. There we were sitting on a bench facing the bar. The Ricards Red tap suddenly turned on all by itself and started spraying beer all over the bar and onto the floor."

During renovations in 2000, Shelly and an employee named Judy shared an experience upstairs. At the time all the doors on the second floor had been removed. The women were sitting in the office, just off the common room. "We heard the door at the top of the stairs open, but there was no door to open! We call this ghost Molly."

Shelly also told me about a light in the dining room alcove that comes on by itself during the night. Betty confirmed that there is activity in that alcove.

One night three weeks before, during the dinner hour, Lisa Muszynski, Kim's sister, and one of the chefs, was standing behind the bar when she watched two glasses hanging from a rack move forward and crash to the floor.

Local historian Reg Thompson came to share some information with us as well. Reg is extremely knowledgeable about the history of the area and has personally researched the murder of Harvey Elliott. Does Reg think the Albion Hotel is haunted?

"I really couldn't say. I haven't seen a glass of beer fly off the shelf, but when it's quiet in the evening and only one or two people are in the pub, sometimes we think someone has just come through the front door. We hear it. The conversation stops. No one comes in to the bar and no one goes out either. You never hear anything else."

Kim has a suggestion to make if you want to book a specific room:

"I had a couple staying in Room 4. It was late at night. I only had one room booked. At 12:30 a.m. we closed the hotel and left for the night. The next morning our guests came down and asked who was playing the guitar downstairs the previous night. They were surprised there was no applause after the playing ended. I checked with all the employees but there had been no one in the building at the time.

"A group of friends and I decided to go down the street after closing time. One of the girls in the group was not feeling well. She decided to retire to Room 4 until we returned. We got back at 2:30 a.m. The poor girl was terrified. She had heard footsteps going back and forth and back and forth in the hallway. She knew she was the only person in the building."

Mike Parkinson, a chef, had an amazing experience one New Year's Eve to suggest otherwise. Mike and Lisa were upstairs after dinner to ready themselves for the New Year's festivities.

"After we did dinner we went up and showered and changed. We were about to come downstairs to join the party. The time was 11:45 p.m. I came out of the room. I opened the door to go downstairs. I saw a figure sitting on the last two steps facing the front door. No one else was in the area. The woman appeared bulky around the shoulder area. Her brunette hair hung down to her shoulders. Her head was bent down. I let go of the door to get Lisa and then I thought 'who was that?'

"I opened the door again, but she was gone. People were now milling around the front hallway. I looked for her in the crowd but she was nowhere to be seen. Then on New Year's Day I was there at the hotel doing the inventory. I know I was not alone in the building."

An interesting cast of characters is in this little village, ghosts and otherwise. It is a gorgeous setting and has a wonderful welcome mat. Should you miss this stop? Not a ghost of a chance!

6

The Secret Guild

N ear the scenic Scarborough Bluffs amid the landscaped gardens, monuments, architectural pieces and original sculptures, stands a two storey chateau called The Guild Inn.

On the surface, The Guild Inn celebrates beauty, leisure and the spirit of creativity. Beneath the surface lies mystery—an underground maze of tunnels that guard the secrets of the decades within their dark passages. These secrets are only hinted at by the eerie and unexpected 'shadows' that make themselves known to those who dare enter.

The property was vacant until Colonel Harold Child Bickford and his family built a summer residence, a pseudo-Georgian chateau in 1914. The original building had it all: servants' quarters, a nursery, a wing for guests and plenty of elegance.

The Guild Inn, 1932

In 1921, Bickford sold the property to Father J.M. Fraser of the China Mission College. It was Father Fraser's dream to train missionaries here, who would then leave for China. In a short time the Father attracted more missionary students then he could accommodate.

He sold the Mission College to Mr. Richard Veech Look, an American businessman, in 1923 for the sum of $50,000. The place was then renamed Cliff Acres but Mr. Look moved on in 1927.

The property remained vacant until 1932, when a

widow named Rosa Breithaupt Hewetson purchased it.

At age 44, Rosa embarked on a new project and a
new marriage at Cliff Acres. Rosa and her husband, Spencer Clark, created what they called a
'guild of all arts.'

The Clarks hoped to make a contribution in those
difficult depression years by stimulating interest in
the arts and crafts and by teaching new ways to
generate a livelihood. Within a year, there were
shops and studios dedicated to sculpture, batik,
hand-loom weaving, tooled leather, ceramics,

Rosa and Spencer Clark.

pewter and copper, wrought-iron and woodwork.

Dining facilities and guest rooms were added until The Guild became a flourishing country inn offering arts and crafts activities.

During the winter of 1942-43, the Clarks were asked by the Canadian government to vacate the entire premises, and The Guild became an official naval base where the first group of Wrens were trained.

The Wrens were stationed in a nearby summer residence named Corycliff. The whole complex was renamed H.M.C.S. Bytown II during the military occupancy and was used to train 50 Wrens as radio operators. The main inn itself was occupied by top military brass.

During the war, Dr. Clarence Finks, head of the Canadian Council of Mental Hygiene, went to England to visit and evaluate a unique hospital called Mill Hill that treated patients with nervous disorders. Upon his return to Canada, he persuaded the government to create this type of facility for its own veterans, and so from 1944 to 1947, The Guild Inn became the hospital Scarborough Hall.

The Clarks got their property back in 1947. But what about the tunnels? When were they built?

Here is part of the mystery. The first house was built in 1914 by a military man and sold soon after World War I. The property was taken over during World War II by the military. Who built the tunnels, and why? What was the military really up to at The Guild during the war?

One tunnel extends just beyond the property to Lake Ontario, perhaps in order to provide secret access or egress from The Guild. This would not have been the first time the military had constructed such tunnels on a lakeshore property in Ontario. For example, no one living in Oshawa during World War II was aware of Camp X, a secret agent training camp. It, too, had a series of buildings connected by underground tunnels linked to Lake Ontario.

The people employed there were sworn to secrecy. Possibly the answer to all this still lies hidden beneath the ground of The Guild.

Krystal Leigh, a paranormal researcher and field investigator who lives on the grounds of The Guild, recalls, "My grandmother talked about working at Corycliff after the war. She said the tunnels extended all around the property. A sliding bookshelf located in Corycliff led to the basement and a tunnel."

Whatever went on in the tunnels, whether it was espionage, top secret medical experiments or simply hidden offices underground to prevent detection, the air was bad, it was dark and the energy was dark and heavy. And that energy imprint has remained.

The Guild Inn in 2003.

When the Clarks regained their home in 1947, some of the former craftsmen returned as well. The Guild's guests and visitors came back in even larger numbers. It was necessary to expand the accommodations and The Guild Inn's reputation grew once more.

The grounds of The Guild are adorned with a collection of historic architectural features. More than 40 years of effort by Spencer Clark resulted in the preservation of fragments of approximately sixty buildings; items like Sir Frederick Banting's fireplace and the original steps of Osgoode Hall are here. A grindstone made in Ireland circa 1860 that was brought to Canada by the Goldie family of Galt is also on the grounds of the Inn.

Spencer was so concerned with preserving Toronto's heritage buildings that he became instrumental in saving Old City Hall from demolition. The grounds of The Guild are literally a monument to his efforts.

Carole Lidgold describes the last years at the Inn for the Clarks. "In 1975, at the age of 87, Rosa had a stroke. She was confined to a wheelchair after the stroke and was no longer able to participate as fully in the activities of the Inn. Spencer suffered from crippling arthritis. He and Rosa knew that their years of owning and managing the Inn were coming to a close.

"For ten years Spencer tried to convince the government of Ontario and Metropolitan Toronto to buy the property. In a statement to the press he said, 'Before I die I want to make sure this place is going to continue. It's my life's work.'

In May of 1978, Metropolitan Toronto council voted to purchase the property." Mel Lastman, later mayor of Toronto, voted against the purchase.

On July 13, 1981, at the age of 93, Rosa Breithaupt Hewetson Clark died. Spencer died of a heart attack on February 11, 1986.

Until the late fall of 2001, The Guild Inn remained open and served as an overnight destination, dining facility and wedding reception centre. Change is now in the wind for The Guild.

The grounds of the Guild Inn feature beautiful classical architecture.

Although the original chateau, or main building, is an historic site, other buildings may be torn down for the future development of a lavish resort. All the items in the inn have been labelled for auction. Fortunately, I was able to tour the grounds and buildings before any demolition or the auction sale had begun.

On September 16, 2001, Krystal Leigh, Sue Derrick, Annette Goodrich, Dee Freedman and Steve Detrich of Hauntings Research Group and their associate Lisa Reid entered the tunnel system of The Guild Inn to conduct an investigation of paranormal activity.

Sue begins, "Steve and I entered the tunnel. The lighting was poor, furnished solely by our flashlight. I immediately pointed out to Steve that I believed there was something in the far corner. It appeared to be a dark, huddled, human-like mass. Annette and Dee entered this room and both immediately and almost in unison stated that there was an 'entity' in the same corner. While Dee maintained her composure, Annette was physically and emotionally shaken by the unfolding experience had started to cry.

"Then my eyes were drawn to an area directly behind Lisa and Krystal. I saw what appeared to be movement, as if someone had entered the tunnel area and was coming toward us. This movement stopped just short of Lisa. As my attention had become solely focussed on this new event, I

One of the remaining open rooms in the Guild Inn tunnel complex. Our author's photograph captured an orb of energy in the left hand corner of the photo and a small one on the right.

did not notice the apparent departure of the entity in the far corner. Whatever it was that had approached us in the tunnel, it was my feeling that it was still there as we left the area."

Dee Freedman, while subsequently staying at the Inn, encountered some uninvited company in her room. "After attending an anniversary party, some of us booked rooms at The Guild for the night. A few of us ended up talking the night away instead of going to bed. At about 5:30 a.m., we heard a loud banging from the room next door. We thought that we might be disturbing our neighbour. As we continued to talk, the doorknob between the suites turned and I said, 'What are they trying to do, get into our room?' at which we all laughed. We later found out that the couple staying in that room had heard the same banging and thought it was us."

By 6:30 a.m. they decided to retire. It was then that Dee encountered a presence. "As I lay down and closed my eyes, a little boy approached me and placed himself right in front of my face. He really wanted my attention and I could not help but notice his unusual eyes—one was brown and the other was blue.

"I was so exhausted that I told him to go away. I immediately fell asleep until 9 a.m. At that time I went across the hall to another room to join the group. While I was sipping my coffee, I described the visit from the little boy earlier that morning. When I mentioned his eyes, I thought one of the girls was going to faint. She said a resident had been having dreams about a little boy with one blue eye and one brown eye."

For several years now, The Guild Inn has closed for the winter months. Krystal Leigh, her husband and young son reside in the inn alone during the winter. They were hired to monitor the grounds and buildings. On February 16, 2002, I joined Dee Freedman, Krystal Leigh, Patrick Cross and Steve Dietrich at The Guild Inn. It was my intention to interview the group and tour the tunnels.

We gathered in a suite on the fourth floor of the inn. We seated ourselves around a coffee table in the living room. Krystal shared her family history and attachment to The Guild, plus a couple of her encounters with spirits.

"At one time an employee working in the prep area of the kitchen heard a bang inside the walk-in fridge. The fridge was always locked. When he went to investigate he discovered the lock had been opened. When he opened the door, he discovered that a box of melons had been knocked over. He cleaned up the mess and relocked the door. A short time later he heard another bang. He turned and saw the fridge lock lying on the floor. He locked it again.

"He went back to his work. Suddenly, he felt someone tugging on a towel that was sticking out of his back pocket. He turned around and saw an apparition. It was a man standing by the doorway to his left. He was wearing a top hat and tuxedo with tails. The spirit walked around a table in the kitchen and then went through a closed door. The employee lost sight of him."

Krystal and her family live on the sixth floor. Krystal had an experience that made her hair stand on end. "I was taking a shower. When I finished, I stepped out and looked at the bathroom mirror. It was fogged up – except for two handprints.

Krystal had other experiences. "My son loves to play with toys. Sometimes you can watch his toys roll across the floor on their own.

"When my son was a baby, I took a picture of him

by the Christmas tree. When I had the photograph developed, it showed him and a misty form standing near him by the tree. When I had the photograph enhanced, the form proved to be a little boy wearing a dress, with long hair."

The most recent occurrence for Krystal was just the week before. "Last Saturday I found my purse floating in the toilet."

As we were all listening, I suddenly got a cold chill down the back of my spine. The feeling left but returned within seconds. I looked around to see if a window was open. This was not the case. Then Patrick said, "We have company." I stared at him. The whole group sat still.

Patrick said, "Dee's camera case, on one of the shelves on the bookcases, is moving up and down." It was true. Patrick pulled out his EMF detector. This device measures the electromagnetic field of an area. The needle started to move erratically back and forth.

Dee said, "We have two spirits in the room with us. One is looking over Terry's shoulder. They are interested in what he is writing." Just as suddenly as they had come, they were gone. On that note, we decided to venture into the tunnels of The Guild.

We took the elevator to the basement. From there we went down a set of stairs into a tunnel. The atmosphere was quite stuffy and heavy. The group remarked how warm it was in the tunnel. It is usually quite cold.

As we walked down the tunnel, Dee caught sight of something running down a side tunnel we had just crossed. I began to look over my shoulder. We entered a small room that contained an old telephone system.

Krystal said, "My mom once saw a female apparition here. She was wearing a navy uniform. She had sharp features with her hair pulled back." Dee sensed something about her and said, "She was a nasty woman. She held a position in the military high command that once occupied the building."

Steve had remained out in the tunnel while we were investigating this room. As we were leaving, he said that he had heard a door close in one of the tunnels. We were not alone.

We re-entered the tunnel system and walked to another room. Dee and Krystal both said that they felt corpses might have been kept there. We didn't linger there for long.

It was time to return to daylight. We ascended to the ground level and walked up to the elevator. Krystal pushed the elevator button. It would not stop at the ground floor. Instead it travelled down to the basement to the tunnels. That was odd. We looked at each other. We waited until it returned to the ground floor. Then the door opened. We stepped inside and wondered who else, or what else, was in there with us.

Hopefully, The Guild Inn will remain a gathering place and a place of great beauty. With the changes that are to be made, the spirits may move on. It is more likely, however, that they will become more active and maybe, just maybe, some secrets will be uncovered about The Guild Inn's unusual past.

7

The Phantom of the
Opera House

Throughout Muskoka many spirits have lingered, to paint, to dance, to act, to canoe along the windswept shoreline. One can sense the magic that permeates Muskoka, a land that has cast its own spell and haunted young and old alike. Here artisans have enjoyed the beauty of nature and water for a century and a half. Many souls refuse to leave only their memories behind.

The first tourists came in 1860 by boat to Washago, and then by stage or foot to McCabe's Landing in Gravenhurst. Alexander Cockburn made Gravenhurst a lake port when he launched the *Wenonah* in 1866, the first, but not the last, steamer on Lake Muskoka.

The Northern Railway was extended to Gravenhurst in 1875. It was a 12 to 14 hour trip from Toronto. A spur line was laid to McCabe's

Landing and there trains were met by the Cockburn company steamers. Tourists could then continue on to Bala or Port Carling and in those days the cottagers stayed all summer.

In 1887, with a population of 2,200, Gravenhurst became a town. Shortly after its incorporation, fire destroyed the entire business district. Although the town promptly rallied to rebuild, fire struck again in 1897 and the Town Hall burned down. By 1901 the magnificent Gravenhurst Town Hall and Opera House was built.

On opening night the *Gravenhurst Banner* printed this account, "The music, songs, choruses and dancing were of the highest standard and most heartily enjoyed by the audience; the whole affair being a huge success. The sale of tickets commenced last Friday at the corner drug store. Considerable interest was at once manifested and, by the time of the show, every reserved seat had been taken. There were 152 seats at 50 cents, 130 seats at 35 cents, and 130 seats at 25 cents. The proceeds of the concert, almost $150, are to be used for stage decorations and the future installation of opera chairs."

In 1934, the Gravenhurst Opera House established the first summer theatre in Canada, thanks to Toronto radio performers John Holden, Isabel Palmer and Babs Hitchmann. They were known as the Good Companions. *The Banner* wrote, "Will Gravenhurst support worthwhile shows? The capacity audience that greeted John Holden and

The Gravenhurst Opera House.

his Good Companions at the Opera House tonight amply demonstrated the answer. The whole company made a decided hit in Gravenhurst."

Canadian-born Holden studied drama in the U.S. May Robson, the actress, encouraged Holden to join the Bonstelle Players of Detroit. Holden performed as an actor for four years, touring small towns and also working on Broadway. When his father died in 1929, Holden returned to Toronto. He ventured into radio and it was at CFRB that Holden rose to prominence. He quickly became a household name when he accompanied Foster Hewitt on his early General Motors' hockey broadcasts.

Cast of children from the opening night of the Gravenhurst Opera House, March 12th 1901.

The Straw Hat Players, a company of outstanding Canadian actors and actresses from all parts of the country, first performed in Gravenhurst on July 21, 1948. One member of this fine troupe was Barbara Hamilton.

From 1948 through 1955, the Straw Hat Players performed 62 different productions at the Gravenhurst Opera House, a total of 308 performances.

Eventually, town officials in Gravenhurst decided to pull up roots and move the town government elsewhere. Gravenhurst researcher J.P. Stratford describes the fate of the Opera House, "Although abandoned by politicians, the now label-confused building remained managed and funded by elected officials as a community property."

A committee was quickly spearheaded by Gordon Sloan to rejuvenate the Opera House. A plan was conceived for upgrading the neglected building.

Between 1969 and 1972, $200,000 was spent refurbishing the Opera House. On September 26th, 1972, the Opera House officially reopened featuring the premiere performance of "Guys and Dolls."

On February 23, 1993, Gravenhurst experienced its darkest day when Ministry of Labour officials padlocked the front doors of the Opera House for safety reasons. An accelerated moisture problem was causing structural damage to parts of the building. It was thought that the building might collapse under a winter snow load. It was estimated that $3,000,000 was needed to restore the structure.

Town officials and caring citizens lobbied the government for financial aid along with their own fundraising incentives. To everyone's amazement, their efforts proved successful. On February 4, 1995, the Gravenhurst Opera House reopened after a classy facelift.

In 1997, the town officials went in search of a town Arts and Culture manager. Ross A.J.Carlin, an entrepreneur and recipient of the Governor-General's Award, created a mission statement for

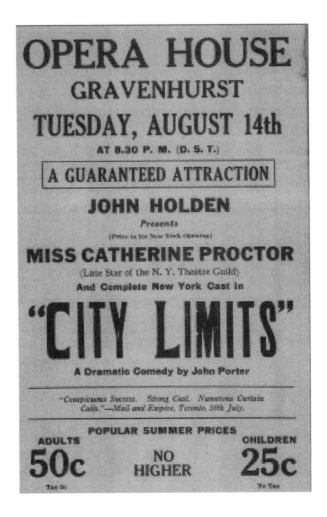

this cultural centre and a high profile image for the Opera House. Today it represents the very best of what Gravenhurst means to its citizens.

Ross was the first person I spoke to about super-natural activity at the Opera House. I asked him if he thought the place was haunted. "Absolutely! I would think that over 100 years of events have given many credible people experiences that are unexplained," he said.

Completely believable but unexplained happenings include sudden door openings, mysterious footsteps, lights turning on and off and being touched by an invisible hand.

"The apparition would eventually be named Ben. Anything and everything to go wrong at the Opera House would eventually become attributed to Ben's ghostly presence," reported the *Banner* newspaper.

Ross feels the spirits are attracted to the energy. "The nature of the building, with so much raw emotional experience, could draw a spirit to it. If I was a spirit I would like to live here."

Although he personally has never seen an apparition, he has certainly had a haunted experience. "In January, 2000, I was working late on a Friday night. I was all alone in the building. When I was ready to leave, I shut my computer off, closed my office door and locked it. I then turned out the lights and locked the front doors as I left the building.

"I was the first person in the Opera House the following morning. The time was about 8 a.m. There was no sign that anyone had entered since I had left the night before. I went to my office and unlocked the door. As I entered, I turned on my computer. When I bent over to turn on the printer, I noticed a piece of paper had been printed during my absence.

"One line had been typed on the page. It read:

'what's happening to me?'

I turned off the computer and the lights and went home!"

Ross also recalled another unexplained experience he had while working in the Opera House. "It was the same month as the computer incident. I was in the process of interviewing a young woman for the job. I took her upstairs to tour the theatre. As we were walking down the aisle toward the stage, I remarked to her that we had a resident ghost. At that moment the chandelier hanging over the stage went on and off several times, right on cue! At the time there was no power turned on in the theatre. I guess that was the spirit's way of saying hello!"

Shortly thereafter, during the Gravenhurst Winter Carnival festivities, American clairvoyant Mary Ellen Rodriguez was asked to try to communicate with the spirits of the Opera House. Ms. Rodriguez was successful.

The Banner newspaper published her results, "Although claiming to identify the presence of numerous transient spirits from the past, the only spirit resident, she said, was an invisible theatre worker, an actor, beside her on the stage, named John."

Subsequent debate has prompted speculation that

The gutted opera house interior

A view from the new stage

A refurbished Opera House stage

the spirit John, may, in fact, be the incarnation of Muskoka summer theatre founder John Holden.

According to the *Banner* newspaper, "The first report of an apparition surfaced around 1960. It was identified as one of the building's construction crew from 1900-01. Apparently distraught following rejection by a young local actress, the Town Hall workman was said to have fallen to his death from the bell tower during construction. The emergence of the unnamed man's ghost was believed to be his unrequited spirit awaiting his true love's stage entrance, an event that would never happen."

Lee Madden has worked as a volunteer at the Opera House during the reconstruction phase and afterwards. One day while working alone in the Opera House, she had an experience.

"I was alone in the building when I suddenly heard someone running below in the back of the building on the first floor. Then a door slammed. The doors in the Opera House are not designed to slam. The door hinges prevent this from happening. I went downstairs to check but no one was in the building. I returned upstairs."

Lee could never have imagined what happened next.

"I felt a cold draft on my back. Then I felt a hand on my shoulder. I turned around but nothing was there. We had often talked about a ghost in the building. We called him Benny, and always blamed him when things went missing. I said, 'Benny, leave me alone. I'm trying to get some work done.' I didn't feel scared."

My third interview was with Dona Rolston whose office was located in the Opera House.

"I believe there is only one spirit in the Opera House. There has been a great deal of speculation as to who the spirit is. I felt the presence was masculine. The sounds made were like someone working with their hands. You could hear the noise of a hammer banging. All the sounds were associated with construction work.

"I also had patrons complain on numerous occasions about cold areas in the building, as though someone was blowing cold air on their shoulders. I heard actors say that they would never get dressed alone in the Opera House. You could always feel a cold breeze coming down the stairs from the second floor."

Early one Saturday morning, Dona encountered the presence of a spirit on the second floor. "At 9 a.m., I arrived at the Opera House. I opened the front door and proceeded to my office located behind the stage. As I entered the office I heard a horrendous crash, like an aluminum ladder falling. I ran out onto the stage. There was nothing there. I thought it was Len, who was the maintenance worker. I called out his name. No one answered.

"I went back to my office and sat down at my desk. I started working but I felt that something was not quite right. It was then that I noticed that someone had turned off my radio.

"Fifteen minutes later I heard the crash again. I went back out and this time I checked the whole building. I was all alone and the Opera House doors were locked. Regardless, I could really feel the presence of someone around me. I returned upstairs and walked out on stage. I said, 'Okay, you obviously don't want me to be here today. Give me a few minutes and I'll be leaving.'"

In July, 2000, the Follows' family arrived in Gravenhurst to star in a one-month production of 'Hay Fever'. They experienced a series of 'happenings' in the Opera House that summer.

The Follows family know the Opera House. Ted Follows was one of the original Straw Hat Players and first acted in the Gravenhurst Opera House in 1952. Gravenhurst researcher J.P. Stratford, writes, "Ted Follows' half-century of acting, directing and producing from coast to coast on radio, television, stage and film is an unbelievable achievement. If there were such a thing as the godfather of Canadian entertainers, Ted Follows would surely head the short list.

"His successes include pages of CBC and CTV roles as well as stage appearances at Stratford, Neptune, and Theatre New Brunswick. However, his children are his proudest legacy. Megan,

Samantha, Edwina and Laurence are all accomplished performers and writers in their own rights."

According to Laurence Follows, Toronto actor and producer of such plays as "Forever Plaid," "Stomp," and "Forever Tango," the Gravenhurst Opera House is indeed haunted.

"During the summer I had heard about the ghost stories. People would joke about them. I hadn't really thought about it or paid any attention to the stories until something happened one night. I was backstage during the third act of the play. It was dark outside by this time. I was near the back stairway when something came around the corner. Then this shadow went down the stairs. I followed it, but there was nothing there."

This was a whole new experience for Laurence at the Opera House. What was that shadow?

More things happened to Laurence during the month of July. He heard unexplained bumps and bangs. The energy in the building seemed heavy. Laurence invited two friends from Toronto, Valerie Farquharson and Leslie Krumins, to come to the Opera House in the hope that they could explain what was going on.

"They toured the basement. One original exposed wall still remains in that part of the building. Valerie walked over and placed her hand on the wall. She started picking up information. She actually tuned into some of the previous council meetings that had occurred here and she sensed trouble.

"She said she opened up a channel and then started closing doorways to allow the trapped energy to flow out. My God, it changed the whole space. A new lightness of energy could be felt on stage."

Valerie had a number of experiences. "There was this entity that would come and go. I also encountered a portal – a doorway or vortex of energy. There were ghosts of theatre people who had been involved in stage productions over the years. I sensed the presence of the builder of the Opera House and the young architect who designed it."

One entity had concerns about the original inspiration for the Opera House. Valerie explained, "The dream was to inspire people to come together. The spirit did not want to ever see the Opera House close. Yet, the spirit was troubled. It was unable to communicate with the living. It was frustrated at not being heard. Each time the spirit attempted to communicate, the spectator would flee. Sometimes as human beings we can mirror our own fears."

I asked Valerie who the spirit was. She replied "John Holden. I can also see a woman near him. She is not always with him. He brings other people in."

When Valerie and Leslie returned they encountered

other spirits who wished to communicate. "We came together on another visit with John Holden and many others...some had been connected directly with him during his time and various others had been connected with the Opera House from its original conception and building, and some of them over the 100 years of its existence.

"The group was like a large council of sorts with John as a major spokesperson. This was important for many of them because of the 100th anniversary of the Opera House and the beginning of a new millennium. They had to find a person or persons who would communicate with them in order to help clear old 'karma' and to assist in creating a new portal for the past to leave through and the new 'transformation' to enter in.

"What occurred during the 6-8 weeks of the summer of 2001 at the Opera House was the beginning of a very positive 'environmental' shift."

No doubt a whole cast of actors and actresses, seen and unseen, will come and go at the Gravenhurst Opera House. No matter what world they belong to, this real world or the world of enchanted Muskoka, you should take it in. When the curtain rises, we might all see something different. The stage is set.

8

The Gananoque Ghost

H e loved it: it was history, it was his family, his power and his prestige. He could not let it go — not for anything — not even death.

Everyone experiences some form of attachment. This yearning for association to a place, a person, or possessions, can begin in youth and sometimes live even beyond the grave.

Charles MacDonald suffered from a yearning attachment. In this case it was to Blinkbonnie, his ancestral home, and he has never left it. He was, after all, the last MacDonald to bare witness to an incredible journey dating back to 1810 in Gananoque, Ontario.

Gananoque is known as the Canadian gateway to the Thousand Islands. The name is a Native word which means both land which slopes toward the water and disappears under it , and place of good health.

The original Gananoque Inn.

One of the first land claims in the area was by Loyalist Joel Stone, who travelled to England in 1783 to petition for compensation for his losses in the American Revolution. Stone arrived in the area in 1787. There were two falls on the Gananoque River and for that reason he requested a land grant on both sides of the river. (He spelled the name of the place Cadanoryhqua and Ganenoquay. In all, there have been 52 variations of the spelling of Gananoque. The present-day spelling first appeared in the 1820s.)

At the same time, Sir John Johnston, leader of a congregation of Loyalists from the Mohawk Valley and a member of the Executive Council, also petitioned for the same land. Johnston was granted 1,000 acres on the east side of the Gananoque River and Stone was granted 700 acres on the west side. The first store, grist mill and tavern were opened in 1792 by Stone.

The next stage of growth did not occur until
Charles McDonald arrived in 1810 from New York
State. He soon became a business partner with
Stone and only one year later he married Stone s
only daughter, Mary.

In 1812, Charles built a new frame home for his
wife. He named his house Blinkbonnie, a Scottish
name meaning good to the eyes or good view.

Charles then persuaded his brother John, of New
York State, to join him in partnership on January
17, 1818, under the firm name C & J McDonald.
By 1824, the brothers had acquired the property
that had originally been granted to Sir John
Johnson on the east side of the river. River power
was now theirs. An east side survey established
the site for the village of Gananoque.

Two years later the McDonalds built the largest
flour mill in Canada. It was estimated that at one
time, one quarter of all the flour sent to Montreal
came from the Gananoque mill.

Unfortunately, Charles McDonald died in 1826 at
the age of 40. A fire destroyed Blinkbonnie the
same year. Charles eldest son, William Stone
MacDonald, (he changed the spelling of his sur-
name) joined the firm in 1833. He resided at
Blinkbonnie with his wife, Isabella Hall, and cared
for his invalid mother during the restoration years.
Blinkbonnie was completely restored by 1843 and
expanded.

Four generations of MacDonalds. From left to right: William Stone (b.1862), William Stone (b 1812) with great-grand-daughter Marion (b.1895) and Charles (b. 1837). Charles may still reside at Blinkboonie.

William and Isabella's son, Charles, was born in 1837 and later became a civil engineer. In 1869 he opened an office in New York City, where he was appointed a trustee in the building of the Brooklyn Bridge. When William Stone MacDonald died in 1902, Charles inherited the property and made extensive renovations to the main house and the surrounding buildings.

When Charles wife died in 1912, he gave his son, William, all the property and securities of the MacDonald family.

Blinkbonnie today, and the entrance to Rebecca's Restaurant.

William, known about town as Mr. Willie, lived in Brooklyn, New York, but spent his summers at Blinkbonnie with his father, Charles. William died of a sudden heart attack in 1920 without a will and all the holdings, including Blinkbonnie, were sold to settle the estate.

His father wept at the prospect of losing the ancestral home. A school teacher named Rebecca Edwards purchased Blinkbonnie in 1923 and proceeded to convert the property into a summer hotel.

Charles MacDonald begged Miss Edwards to allow him to take up residence at his beloved Blinkbonnie for his remaining years. She was delighted.

During her tenure Miss Edwards lovingly restored as much of the original Blinkbonnie furniture as she could find.

She even searched for some of the family antiques that had been sold to furnish his living quarters. Those she could not find she replaced with equal age and style.

Charles, restored to his original home, was a fortunate and happy man. He died in 1928 but many feel he never did leave Blinkbonnie.

Blinkbonnie s reputation as one of the finest hotels in the Thousand Islands spread far and wide. This fame was deserved, for the accommodation was excellent and the grounds and gardens were breathtaking.

Miss Edwards was very particular in her care of each guest room. She continued to restore and refine Blinkbonnie with fine linens, beautiful china and period lamps and figurines.

The staff were all well trained and encouraged to feel like part of the family. All the MacDonald buildings were eventually converted to guesthouses, as well as the adjacent carriage houses and cottages.

Miss Edwards determination to maintain this level of excellence finally cost her the hotel because she did not have the means to maintain it after her retirement from teaching. Blinkbonnie was sold in 1957, divided into private homes and was passed to many successive owners. It became a dark shadow of its former self.

Only Charles remained, a witness to the sad changes. Did Rebecca Edwards choose to stay as well? Did her years of ownership and love of Blinkbonnie hold her to it?

In 1983, the Seal family purchased the historic inn. Their intent was to restore the 19th century building and property to its former glory.

Today the Blinkbonnie Harbour Inn features 50 units, including whirlpool suites, a bistro restaurant, a pool and an English-style pub. The convention facilities can accommodate up to 120 people.

Derek is the maintenance supervisor. He has spent the last 13 years taking care of the building, the property and the guests of the inn — and perhaps Charles himself.

I often hear footsteps and doors opening and closing, and sometimes I can hear a woman singing in the lounge area, said Derek. Of course no one is to be seen.

A few years ago, Derek encountered a man at Blinkbonnie who claimed to be a psychic. According to him, he could sense the presence of a man, a woman and a little girl. For years, people have acknowledged the presence of Charles MacDonald s spirit. But who could the woman and the little girl be?

Miss Edwards is thought to be the woman, possibly too attached to leave. After all, she put her heart and soul into Blinkbonnie. As for the little girl, no one seems to know.

The third floor of Blinkbonnie has not been used for several years. Water and electricity is shut off to this level. One night after closing time, Derek was making his final rounds of the building when he heard water running. Oddly enough, the sound was coming from the third floor. Derek and a fellow employee named Mark started up the stairs. Yes, there was water running somewhere on the third floor. How could this be when the water was shut off to this level?

The men soon discovered where the sound was

coming from — the bathroom on the third floor.
Then it stopped.

They entered cautiously. The bathtub was full of
water. And there was something even more bizarre
about the tub full of water there was no stopper
in the tub.

Mark is quite familiar with Blinkbonnie. He grew
up across the street from the inn. In the fall of
1985, he started to work full-time at Blinkbonnie
as a bus boy.

 I worked as a waiter, night man, bartender, maintenance person and finally, assistant manager. I
lived up on the third floor for two years in 1987-
88. In those days the inn closed down for the winter and I would be the only person residing in the
building.

He has much to relate about ghostly activity.

 Once, in the middle of the night, I heard this loud
crash in the bathroom. I sat up. I decided to
check it out. When I entered the bathroom, I discovered the glass globe that covered the ceiling
light bulb had crashed to the floor and broken.
The light bulb was screwed in and intact. You
would have to unscrew it in order for the globe to
fall to the floor.

 On another occasion I awoke to the sound of a
splash against the window. It sounded like someone had thrown a snowball at the glass. I got up
and peeked out the curtain. There was snow on

the ground but no footprints.

In 1985, employees of the Federal Health and Welfare Department booked a number of rooms at Blinkbonnie for a holiday. These guests had more in mind than pure relaxation. They had a Native psychic with them.

Their intention was to conduct a s ance during the weekend. At the time, Mark was working as a bartender. He told me what happened.

The group decided to hold the s ance in room 302. They had brought a ouija board with them. During the s ance, the Native woman saw the figure of Charles MacDonald appear in the room.

The weirdest thing about this session was when the Native woman saw the ghost of a young girl appear next to her but the girl was part of their group and still very much alive. The poor girl fled the room and rushed down to where I was at the bar. She was mortified. Did this mean she was going to die? The whole experience was never explained.

Although Mark is no longer employed at Blinkbonnie, he will never forget the unexplained experiences he encountered while working there.

Charles MacDonald is likely to remain at Blinkbonnie forever, after all, it was his most beloved home. Are any of us likely to find such a suitable place, and if we do, would we want to leave it either?

9

The Hockey Hall of Infamy

T hey were trustworthy individuals, handling other people's money every day, but they gambled dangerously with their own lives. They worked together at a beautiful old bank at Yonge and Front Streets in Toronto.

First constructed in 1885 during a period of prosperity and optimism in Canada's future, the Bank of Montreal marked the rise of commerce and an age of decadence. In its day, it was the largest bank branch in Canada. The building is a florid example of rococo architecture and was designed by the Toronto firm Darling and Curry. It served as the head office of the Bank of Montreal until 1949 and then as a branch office until 1982, when it was closed permanently.

The central hall measures 70 feet by 70 feet (21metres x 21 metres) and rises 45 feet (13 metres) to a stained glass dome. The dome is the largest of its kind in Toronto. It was constructed by Joseph McCausland and Sons and features 24 fanned panels that depict allegorical dragons guarding gold from eagles. Around the outside are cornucopia filled with fruit and flowers. In the centre, circles bear emblems representing the provinces of Canada.

The detail in the hall is exquisite. The framing of the mezzanine on the west side that once served as the boardroom is incredible. The bank manager's private apartment was located just behind the mezzanine. Outside, an octagon reflects the interior, diagonal corner arches. To the left of the south portico, a huge stone figure of Hermés stands. He has supported the weight of the building's chimney on his shoulders for all these years. Massive, arched plate glass windows indicate the size of the interior.

It was the perfect setting for romance to blossom, and blossom it did.

Her name was Dorothy. This attractive woman worked as a teller in the bank, and she was the most popular girl on staff. Her handsome lover was also employed as a bank teller. They had to keep their liaison a secret. Not only were they co-workers—he was already married. If anyone suspected their love they could both lose their jobs.

Their fellow workers were starting to smile at them differently. Some of the women quit speaking, as if interrupted, when Dorothy entered the room.

And then something snapped. Her lover broke it off—a change of heart and Dorothy was cast aside.

Devastated by his betrayal, she slipped into a state of deep depression. Hurt, humiliated, fearful that her former friends at the bank knew her shame, Dorothy still had to go to work every day.

One morning in March of 1953, she entered the bank at 7 a.m., went up to the women's washroom on the third floor and remained there for some time.

When he was interviewed by *Toronto Star* journalist Stefan Scaini, Len Redwood, chief messenger for the bank, recalled seeing Dorothy that morning. "It was much earlier than she was expected to be in. She looked pretty rough, probably had had a night out." A night out or a sleepless night?

She returned downstairs for a brief time, and then went upstairs again. Redwood described what happened, "The next thing I heard was a shot."

Dorothy had taken the bank's own revolver and shot herself in the head.

In those days, each bank had at least one gun; employees were expected to shoot it out with robbers. Her death sent shock waves through the employees and, no doubt, her former lover.

Unexplained things began to happen immediately. The lights in the bank would go on and off by themselves. Locked doors were discovered to be wide open.

Redwood admitted, "We all felt something. There

was someone watching us but you couldn't see anyone. The cleaning staff became nervous about
working in the bank after dark, claiming they heard
funny noises. The women refused to use the
upstairs washroom, so the bank was forced to build
another one in the basement."

Over forty years later, on June 18, 1993, the Hockey
Hall of Fame opened the doors of its current home
in this magnificently restored Bank of Montreal.
The main mission of the organization is to collect
and preserve objects and images connected with the
game of hockey.

A second objective is public education about the history and rules of play of this great Canadian game.
Schools, tourists and hockey fans alike tour the
facilities on a daily basis. Visitors enjoy the many
exhibits on display, including the hall of hockey's
finest players. In the first year of operation, more
than 500,000 people visited the building.

In 1993, William Houston of the *Globe and Mail*,
wrote, "The new Hockey Hall of Fame in Toronto has
just about everything, including a ghost. The ghost
is Dorothy and she resides in the restored Bank of
Montreal building that is part of the new Hall at
BCE Place."

"Over the years, custodians of the bank have heard
shrieking and moaning noises coming from the
rooms. Items have gone missing or have been
moved. Christine Simpson, who is in charge of pub-
licity at the new Hall, says, "If we've misplaced

something we say, 'Well, it must be Dorothy.' "

Recently, a gentlemen and his young son arrived to tour the hockey exhibits. After proceeding through the lower concourse level they entered the building proper. Directly ahead of them just to the left was an elevator; the elevator door was open. The son stood staring fixedly at the elevator doorway as he watched the ghost of a pretty, young woman beckon him to enter. Seconds later the door closed and travelled up to the third floor.

For half a century Dorothy has remained behind. She gambled everything for love—and she lost.

The Lonely Ghosts of Fort George

A musket in hand, a sentry paces the grounds of Fort George, a British fortification on the Niagara frontier. He awaits the second American assault. Below, American warships take up their position on the Niagara River. This invasion could begin at any moment. As he turns towards the strategic artillery battery to his right, a thick haze of mist begins to drift in, obscuring his view. When it clears, the soldiers are gone and the battle is over. Strangely-dressed people are passing him by.

He is a casualty of time, not war.

1811 saw an aggressive America demanding immediate invasion of British North America. Henry Clay, a strong opponent of Great Britain, was confident that an easy victory across the border was as good as done. "I trust I shall not be presumptuous when I state that I verily believe that the militias of Kentucky alone are competent to place Montreal and Upper Canada at your feet."

Clay estimated it would be all over in a short four weeks.

In February of 1812, Congress ordered the organization of a volunteer army of 50,000 men. Four months later the United States declared war on Britain.

Although Great Britain did send some regular military forces to Upper and Lower Canada, their numbers were few in comparison to the American forces. Meanwhile, the presence of the British military on the Niagara Peninsula under the gallant commander-in-chief, Major-General Isaac Brock, fostered a sense of security.

As a result of the Jay's Treaty back in 1794, Great Britain had been given two years to vacate their defensive works within the boundaries of the United States. By 1796 they had abandoned Fort Niagara and crossed the Niagara River into Upper Canada. Over the next three years the British built Fort George just outside Newark, now called Niagara-on-the-Lake, the capital of Upper Canada at the time. The fort was constructed on a small rise overlooking the river and the British naval base.

On the morning of October 13, 1812, the famous Battle of Queenston Heights was fought. Major

General Sir Isaac Brock had been busy preparing Upper Canada as well as he could against attack. After he defeated the Americans at Detroit, General Brock quickly left for the Niagara River frontier where only 1500 men stood guard against attack.

On the night of October 12th, General Brock rested at Fort George. Just after midnight, the American forces crossed the river at Queenston. Was this the Americans' main attack or a diversion to draw the British forces from Fort George? Brock's second-in-command, General Sheaffe, and the main British force were left behind at Fort George.

The General met a messenger along the road who had news that a great number of the enemy had already crossed the river and more were coming. Brock sent the messenger to Fort George to bring General Sheaffe and his troops along as quickly as possible.

Queenston village was situated at the foot of Queenston Heights, a steep cliff rising some 350 feet from the edge of the Niagara River. The British had strategically placed a gun at the top of the Heights. The Americans came up behind the British gunners by a steep and narrow path. Taken by surprise, the British beat a hasty retreat.

General Brock understood the seriousness of the situation and did not wait for General Sheaffe, but, instead, rallied a small force and charged up the steep hill, sword drawn!

Although he broke the ranks of the American force, he was struck down himself. Suddenly, the British lines faltered and retreated to the foot of the hill with their fatally wounded leader.

General Sheaffe had just arrived and took command. He ordered his troops to strike inland. Led by Native guides, Sheaffe managed a surprise attack on the flank of the Americans. Although the Americans had a sizeable force that outnumbered their opposition, they panicked and tried to escape. American troops still on their own side of the river were ordered to cross, but refused. Those on the Newark side rowed, swam back or drowned; the remainder surrendered to the British.

The spring of 1813 saw better-trained American forces at the front and they were ready to launch yet another major invasion. On 25th of May, hundreds of American cannons opened fire on Fort George. The casualties were enormous and by morning Fort George was a smoldering rubble of destruction. The remaining garrison force fled to safety. American forces, under the cover of a morning fog, crossed the river and landed on British soil.

The British retreated to Hamilton and eventually managed to halt the onslaught at Stoney Creek and Forty Mile Creek. The Americans were forced to retire back to Niagara.

American Army engineers quickly refortified Fort

Fort George re-enactments

George. They even dug up the cemetery of St. Marks's Anglican Church in order to enlarge their fortifications. The poor townspeople of Newark were at the mercy of the invading force and anyone sympathetic to the enemy was jailed.

By December, British forces had rallied and advanced on Niagara. The Americans abandoned the district and retired across the river. They torched Niagara first and only two buildings out of 150 remained by morning.

The British re-occupied Fort George, and later attacked and captured Fort Niagara on the American side. On December 24th, 1814, the

Treaty of Ghent ended the War. The Americans had lost against the British.

In the late 1820's Fort George was abandoned by the military and fell into ruin. The cavalry did stable here during the Rebellion of 1837. However, by the time of Confederation in 1867 the fort was in total disrepair. Locals had even dismantled buildings for firewood, and eventually the military establishment became the site of a farmer's field.

During the 1930's the Niagara Parks Commission completely restored Fort George to its former glory. Since 1969, Parks Canada has administered the fort as a national historic site.

Today Fort George is seen by some as an historic destination. Some visitors, however, see more than that. They see the dead who once occupied this site prior to and during the War of 1812. A wide range of phenomena haunts the Fort, from rapping, knocking, cold spots, footsteps, to moaning, crying, scents and strange breezes. Many people experience overwhelming feelings of terror, sorrow, anguish and nausea. The psychokinetic phenomena includes piano playing, furniture moving, doors shutting, doors opening, poking and playing with people's hair. These are simply evidence of far more important phenomena.

Kyle Upton conducts ghost-walk tours of the fort. "I have been running the Ghost Tours through Fort George since 1994. When I started, I believed in ghosts, but that belief has changed considerably

Blockhouses 1,2,and 3 at Fort George.

Blockhouse 1

due to my experiences through the years. I have heard things, I have felt things and I have seen things. Sometimes I have been more surprised than the people I'm guiding and sometimes I am afraid."

By 1999 Kyle had toured 8,000 people through Fort George. That same year he published ghostly accounts in a book entitled NIAGARA'S GHOSTS AT FORT GEORGE.

The tour begins at the front gates and passes by the sentry box, the cottage, Brocks-Bastion, Blockhouse 1 and Blockhouse 2, the Officer's Quarters, the guardhouse, the sawpit and the woodyard. Straight ahead is the Artificer's Building, the Officers Quarters kitchen and the Powder Magazine. The Powder Magazine, ironically, is the only original building to survive the War of 1812.

Past the magazine is the tunnel entrance extending some 70 feet (22 metres) underground and connecting to the Octagonal Blockhouse. It is here, in this tunnel, that people see shadowy figures and hear footsteps. It is not uncommon for people to flee the tunnel and run for the front gates after an experience.

Heather Baures of California visited the Fort on Sunday, June 11, 2000, and told me of her experience.

"The tunnel curves, so I was unable to see the tour

guide, who had the only light in the dark tunnel. I got the impression that someone was standing behind me. When I turned around, I could see the entrance to the tunnel, which was only a gray rectangle of moonlight. On either side of the tunnel, there were two men. The one on the right stepped forward and extended his arm towards the other man. After holding it there a moment, he stepped back and dropped his arm to his side. He then knelt down and leaned forward. It looked like he was picking up something. I could tell the men were wearing late-eighteenth century clothing and

Fort George Tunnel

the one on the right was wearing a tricorne hat. I believed in ghosts before I went to Fort George; now my beliefs are definitely confirmed."

Barb Cole of Toronto has been on the ghost tour three times. On her first tour she and her husband heard many things but nothing actually happened. On the second tour with her children, something did.

"My children and I were visiting the fort in the daytime after having taken the ghost tour the night before. It was in the afternoon, a time not as busy as the morning that we toured the fort. We had gone through the tunnel and up the lookout. We

Officer's Complex at Fort George

were the only ones there at that time.

"We came back through the tunnel when my 14-year-old son saw a white, shadowy figure on the wall in the back of the tunnel where we had just been. It looked to me like a large spot on the wall, perhaps a patch of daylight, but after a few minutes it formed into the shape of a man. It ran to the other side of the tunnel where it vanished. I could not see facial features but I saw a human shape with arms and legs. It was all white."

Kyle tells of a visitor who fled the fort after her experience. On that visit, as the woman exited from the tunnel, she noticed that the electric lights behind her went out, and she remarked upon this to her friend. Her friend didn't know what she was talking about. She thought the lights were on.

"She saw three shadowy figures materialize from this 'solid cloud of shadow'. These three male figures, who wore tall hats, (she believed that they were soldiers from the War of 1812) then began moving towards her and the entrance to the tunnel. As they came closer, she turned about and fled from the fort as fast as she could go, dragging her astonished friend."

After the tour is finished Kyle is left alone in the fort. It is usually near midnight. It is then that he becomes uncomfortable.

"At night, the fort can be an intimidating place even for those of us familiar with it. There are some nights when it even gets to me. The atmosphere of the fort changes from that of a tourist attraction to that of a churchyard. The air thickens to the point of oppressiveness, and a haze settles into the corners of your vision, only to vanish as you turn to confront it."

It was during one of these nights that Kyle saw something.

"As I sped to escape from what had become a less-than-comfortable Fort George, I looked into the lit window of Blockhouse 1, only to find its light blocked by the shadowy form that filled the portal.

The staircase of Blockhouse 2.

Now I had seen ghosts before, and I'm not spooked
easily, but while other ghostly experiences had
been curious sensory phenomena, this one hit me
at a purely emotional level. I was filled with such
a feeling of terror that I contemplated climbing
over the high wooden palisades to escape from the
fort, rather then risk walking past that building to
the front gate. In all my life, only nightmares have
imparted the same incredible sense of fear."

The most haunted blockhouse and the largest is
number 2. This structure contains the supply
depot and barracks and has a staircase in the
middle leading to an upper floor. The spirit of a
man inhabits the second floor of the building. On
one occasion two guides encountered this phantom
walking across the second floor room. Initially one

The Officer's Kitchen.

guide who was preparing to close the building for the night caught sight of this gentleman when he was standing at the top of the stairs. Repeated requests asking the gentleman to follow him down-stairs failed. The guide then approached the man. However, he continued to move away until he was cornered in the room. At that precise moment the guide was just reaching out to touch the man, when his partner arrived at the top of the stairs and spoke to him. He turned to answer his friend and explain what was happening. As soon as he did this, the man he had cornered disappeared from sight. During another tour of duty at closing time they heard the man's footsteps upstairs.

Kyle tells of one intriguing encounter in

Blockhouse 2 in his book. A woman and her son visited the Blockhouse. While the woman was conversing with the guide, her seven-year-old son wandered about the barracks. Soon he was talking aloud in the back corner of the room. The mother took little notice until it was time to leave. Her son refused to go. The guide, sensing something unusual, asked him who he was talking to. The boy answered "the man." He then described the man as the same height as the guide and wearing the same kind of red military uniform. He wore the same red coat with long tails, however, it had yellow stripes on the cuffs and collars instead of green stripes like the guide's uniform.

Kyle explained, "Now any good historian knows that the British army colour coded its soldiers. Every Regiment of troops had a distinctive colour for the 'facings' or cuffs and collars of their uniforms. While historians may be aware of this fact, most seven-year-olds are not. Nor are most seven-year-olds aware of the fact that the 100th Regiment, along with their yellow-faced coats, were stationed at Fort George just before the War of 1812."

The boy said the man was very unhappy. The poor fellow had no idea how he had ended up in the barracks, or where all his friends had gone. He was frustrated that no one would talk to him or even look at him. He was also angry with all the people coming and going through his home.

The Officers' Quarters facing the parade square in

the centre of the fort is probably the eeriest of all –
not for the faint-hearted.

The officers who once occupied the building lived
here like gentlemen. They attempted to recreate in
their living quarters the high material and social
standards they were accustomed to in Great
Britain.

The building is laid out to reflect its original
appearance. As you enter the front door a sitting
room is located on the right side. The central part
of the structure was the dining area and then a
games room and personal quarters. These reflect-
ed the background, rank and interests of the officers.

Dinners were sophisticated affairs, complete with
fine silverware and china, serving dishes and
decanters of port and sherry. The Officers' Kitchen
was located at the back of the building. Here staff
would prepare elaborate full-course dinners.

The female employee who first greeted me at the
main gate mentioned two areas known to be
haunted; one is the Officers' Quarters. "I will not
go near Blockhouse 1 at night nor the Officers'
Quarters. When you walk by the windows of the
Quarters you get an eerie feeling like someone is
watching you."

According to some staff and visitors' the mirror
hanging in the sitting room contains the ghostly
image of a woman. This female spirit is described

as having long, slightly curly hair. Although the gilt-framed mirror dates back to the 1790's it is not an original furnishing of Fort George. No one knows who she is. In recent years, she has been seen outside of the mirror. One young child on a tour said she wore a "Cinderella dress" and had slightly curly hair, which she had been brushing with a silver palm hairbrush.

In 1981 during major repairs to the Officers' Quarters the building was left with gaping holes for a period of time. Four staff members volunteered to sleep over in the barracks of the fort and maintain the security of the site. It was midnight and they had just settled down in their sleeping bags when they heard banging and crashing noises coming from the Officers' Quarters.

Kyle said, "Rushing outside to see what was the matter, they hurried into the building that they were supposed to be guarding. They had arrived too late; there was no one in sight, but some of the furniture on display in the Senior Officers' wing had been moved around. The puzzled staff relocated the out-of-place objects. They decided to shift their bunk-space into the sitting room on the far side of the building. When the noises began anew, the four guardians took only seconds to rush into the Senior Officers' wing. They arrived in time to see the furniture still in the process of being rearranged, dishes sliding across the wooden tables by themselves, armchairs propelled around the room by unseen hands. Stopped in their tracks, they stared in aghast astonishment for a

minute, and then fled, screaming, from the building."

The gift shop, located at the back of the fort, was
the site of the kitchen for the hospital building
next door. It is now the craftsman's shop or
Artificer's Shop. However, the original building
also served as a charnal house where terminally ill
patients from the hospital were placed. There they
awaited their death in the damp cellar area
beneath the kitchen.

A place where you could lose sight of your own
soul. In fact, many patients did. They remain
there, waiting to see the light.

The only written account of an experience in this
building happened like this: a couple using the
washrooms on the side of the building heard the
sound of footsteps above them. The building has
no second storey today but a painting hanging in
Blockhouse 1, by a military surgeon stationed in
Niagara before the War of 1812, shows the original
building had a second storey.

Many people experience a sense of sadness inside
and outside the Gift and Artificer's shops. One
employee working in the Artificer's shop stated,
"This was the site of a 60-bed hospital. Many visitors experience a sense of pain and illness. Many
of the dismembered arms and legs were buried
just outside the back of this building."

Other tourists have reported seeing a man dressed

in white standing near the buildings. Could he have been a surgeon?

No matter where you go inside this Fort you are bound to confront spirits and smell an odd odour, see a reflection in a mirror, watch a table move by unseen hands, see a building that no longer exists or hear a piano playing in the sitting room of the Officers' Quarters.

I highly recommend that you join Kyle Upton on a ghost walk sometime. It could change your life, or, you could be one of those strangely-dressed people who ignore the poor sentry at the gate.

Readers' Response

One of the most wonderful aspects of being a writer is reader response. When it comes to writing ghost stories the reader response is not only incredible, but worth printing. Many people have stories of their own to share.

Thank you, to everyone who has written to me, for your leads and marvelous words and the generosity to take the time to write your stories. In honour of your efforts, here are a few I'd like to share with you.

Haunted Church

Dear Mr. Boyle;

I first read your two books of Ontario ghost stories last October when we were visiting relatives in Bracebridge. I thought at the time of writing to you but didn't. On rereading your books this week, I decided to write. I found them both fascinating.

I have always been interested in the supernatural, and have collected "ghost" stories all my life, but I never had a personal experience with the supernatural until 1994.

My wife of 27 years died suddenly in March that year and I was deeply depressed. Later that spring, a colleague at the Canadian Museum of Civilization, where I had worked, suggested that we visit Stratford. He stayed at a B & B (which turned out to be run by one of my wife's elementary school teachers) and I stayed with a friend who was the minister at the old Presbyterian church near the land registry office.

There are two Presbyterian churches in downtown Stratford; this is the older of the two. It is a huge, labyrinthine building, which has had several additions over the years, hence has many levels and corridors.

My friend explained to me that the church had been built on the site of a cemetery. All the graves that were known were moved, but there were a number of unmarked graves, including those of some murderers hung at the county gaol, which occupied part of the site. When excavation began, human remains were unearthed.

The church is reputed to be haunted and he told me that, several times over the years, he had heard people walking and in some cases running on the floor over his office, when he was working there at night. On searching the church, he had found nothing. On one occasion, he was working in his office at night when he heard footsteps come down the hall towards it. He looked at the door and saw the door knob turn. He jumped up and opened the door, but there was nothing there.

I found all this interesting and very credible, as my friend is a pretty hard-headed individual, not given to fantasy.

One of the church officers was there when we arrived. We conversed for a few moments, then he left. My friend made sure the door was locked behind him, then proceeded to take me on a tour of the church. We were about three levels up, in the tower, where he was showing me their sound system, when the fire alarm went off. We hastened back to his office, where he called the fire department to report that we were in the church but could see no evidence of fire.

While he was on the telephone, I was standing outside his door and noticed that the fire alarm on the wall next to his door had been pulled and that the little glass bar was lying on the floor, in two pieces. I called this to his attention while we waited for the fire department. As the door near his office was still locked, we had to admit the firemen, who were accompanied by a police officer.

With them, we checked every room in the church, tried every door, they were all locked, and every window, likewise. There was no explanation for the fire alarm. After the firemen had left, we made a second inspection with the police officer. We were all perplexed. When she asked what she was supposed to put in her report, my friend said, "Well, I strongly suggest you don't attribute it to the ghosts!"

The Scent of Perfume

As I said, my dear wife's death depressed me profoundly, but I must say that I have never once questioned the reason for her death. I have always felt that God had a purpose in it. That has not made me less sad and lonely. Some weeks following her death, I was feeling very low. I went into our bed-

room, sat down on her side of the bed and wept. Suddenly the air was filled with the scent of her perfume. It was VERY striking. I sat there amazed for perhaps a minute, then left the room and immediately re-entered it. The scent was gone.

My daughter and my wife's sisters had cleaned out all my wife's clothes and other belongings, including her perfume, WEEKS before. No drawers had been opened and I had done absolutely nothing that could account for the scent of her perfume.

I may say that I felt very close to my wife at that moment, if astounded, and was very comforted. It was as if she had come to reassure and comfort me. In the next two years, I had four or five similar experiences, always in the same place except on one occasion when I was walking to the bus stop, on a route she had taken many times walking to a nearby mall, and I smelled her perfume outdoors. The closest person was perhaps 100 yards away and was down wind from me. Each time, the scent seemed weaker than the previous.

Some months went by and I assumed I would not smell the scent again. In April 1997, I had been on a trip to France and Belgium and I returned home. My children had moved out by now, both our dogs were dead, and I came home to a very quiet house. I went into the bedroom and said out loud, "Well, Brenda, I'm home!" Suddenly, but faintly, I smelled the perfume.

I have only smelled it once since then. In May 1998,

a lady whom I met, moved in with me. In June 1999, my daughter, who had a very special, close relationship with my wife, was married. It was a wonderful wedding and the reception, at the National Arts Centre, was spectacular. My companion and I returned home following the reception. Sue was somewhere else in the house. I was in the bedroom, sitting on my side of the bed and I was thinking, "Oh, Brenda, if only you could have been there!" And there was the perfume again, light and fleeting, only for a few seconds. I have not smelled it since.

Larry Needham

The Donnelly Homestead

Dear Mr. Boyle;

My wife and I have long enjoyed your 'Discover Ontario' radio program and yesterday we bought your book HAUNTED ONTARIO. To be perfectly frank I'm a bit of a skeptic when it comes to the paranormal but the index entry of six pages on the Donnellys caught my attention. I have had a 30-year fascination with the Donnelly story during which time I had many talks with Ray Fazakas, the author of THE DONNELLY ALBUM,, and corresponded for a while with Nora Lord who was William Donnelly's daughter and who died in Sudbury on 22 September, 1975 at age 88.

In June 1997 we paid a visit to Rob and Linda Salts' place on the Roman Line. We did the tour of the property, something I had wanted to do for years but the previous owner was hostile to the idea of visits from strangers and kept the property posted.

Rob, who claims to be a psychic, certainly has no

doubts about the presence of spirits in his home and barn. And something happened while we were there to shake my scepticism, at least somewhat.

On page 86 of your book you relate that people touring the site often mention that something touched them on the shoulder while no one was standing near them. I had a similar experience. While Rob was leading us from the house to the murder scene, I felt something brush across the top of my head. My first thought was that a flying insect, a very large flying insect had got into my hair. I patted the top of my head very gingerly so as to dislodge it without getting stung, but there was nothing there. Then the same thing happened again. This time I ran the fingers of both hands through my hair but came up with nothing. I didn't mention this to anyone at the time but a week or two later I wrote to Rob telling him about it.

Bill Burns

The Hauntings of Queen's University Radio Station

Dear Mr. Boyle:

I received your HAUNTED ONTARIO for Christmas, and my holidays are now spoken for. It's well written, and fun. My wife bought it for me, as she knows I love Ontario history.

Can someone haunt a radio transmitter? This doesn't involve spectres or ghostly figures, but it does strongly suggest communication from beyond. Your story of Mr. E.B. Sutton, Bala Bay Hotel, prompted the memory, with his knockings on the hotel front door.

Before I go on, I should say that I really don't believe in spirits, ghosts, or things that go bump in the night. In fact, I hold no superstitions, and think most of this haunted stuff is bunk. Granted, some interesting things have happened, so I maintain an open mind. I certainly don't have an explanation for what happened in your book. Nor what happened to me at CFRC.

Queen's University established the second radio sta-

tion in Canada in 1923. They have published a book describing its history, however, the key thing to know is that it all started as an experiment in the electrical engineering department. Radio broadcasting was in its infancy then, and Queen's EE was on the forefront when they built a transmitter and went on the air. They broadcast from Fleming Hall, from a room on the upper floor. Two professors and a graduate student started the station. Professor D.M. Jemmett was the key person, who had the idea and got things going.

By the time I graduated in 1974 from Electrical, CFRC was fifty years old, and Professor Jemmet had retired, and was in poor health.

The station still operated its transmitter on the second floor of Fleming Hall, with the antennas on the roof. This has all since been replaced.

I was the station engineer, although it was largely a voluntary job involving starting the transmitters, and checking them regularly. I took it quite seriously, though, as I was a keen ham operator, and had worked as engineer at CHFI, CFTR and CBC. I liked working with the old 1946 RCA transmitter, and knew its gut intimately.

The fall of 1975 saw me in graduate studies in Electrical, and volunteering as station Engineer and doing some announcing. Late on Thursday night, I returned to my downtown apartment late to get a cup of tea, and wind down from an evening studying on campus. It was your classic dark and stormy night, *with a cold wind and rain. When I got a call from Mary Lou Keating at the station I was not too keen on getting on my bicycle, and heading back to campus. However, she said that the AM signal was off the air, the original CFRC was AM of course, while FM soldiered on.*

It was about 12:15 a.m., but I was keen enough to go back and let myself in to a dark Fleming Hall. This place was built in the 1800's and was spooky even in the daytime. On the third floor the transmitter room was dark, and sure enough, the AM set was off the air. The power was on, and all the tubes were glowing, but it was deader than dead. I opened it up, and could find no fault. The set had tripped off by itself, and just wouldn't start. After about an hour, I still couldn't reset it, so headed home. Working on high voltage alone at night is never a good idea, and this big old RCA was not cooperating.

The next morning, I arrived before my first class, only to find that all classes were cancelled that morning. No explanation. I used the time profitably to find the fault in the AM transmitter. It took three hours and it was a real sleuth job. Despite being an experienced transmitter engineer, this fault was the hardest, and weirdest that I had seen. An insulated wire, buried deep in the guts, had been pushed up against a high voltage terminal. The insulation had been burned off, and the two were welded together. This could only happen if you had the power on, and were rubbing one against the other. No person could do this, as the power would go off once you opened the doors. For the life of me, I couldn't figure out why it would hap-

pen, let alone after thirty years of loyal service.

I closed everything back up, and made things ready to go back on the air. Finally emerging from the transmitter room, I learned the reason for the class cancellations. The night before, about 11:30 p.m., Professor Jemmett had died at Kingston General Hospital. KGH is across the quadrangle from Fleming Hall.

Being curious, I ran the logger tape back. This tape recorder takes its audio feed from a radio receiver, and would show the time of disruption. At 11:56 p.m. Mary Lou gave a time check. Four minutes later, the tape went dead.

A bizarre fault, at midnight, on the eve that Professor Jemmett died. I don't know. Sounds spooky to me. It's not just the timing that gets me; it's that no human hands could have created that fault, unless they were already inside the transmitter cabinet, which is not possible.

Ian Baines

P.S. One evening I was returning to my room in Northern France, and crossed an old First World War battlefield. I had been to many such places, and they hold no fear for me. However, as darkness fell, I was aware of hundreds of other people around me. My skin went cold, and I had to fight the urge to run. There was nobody there, just a dark woods with old trenches and wire. But, I'll tell you, I was not alone on that field. There was no doubt in my mind of that. That kind of makes me wonder.

Two Haunted Houses

Dear Mr. Boyle:

I have two stories to relate to you: a haunted house in Port Hope, and a haunted school in Whitby.

The Haunted House in Port Hope—

A house on Dorset Street in Port Hope, is quite haunted. At one point a man is said to have murdered his family in the home. I have heard this took place around 1870, but I would hesitate to put money on the year.

I have been told that the house was constructed back in the 1800's sometime. It was possibly the servants' quarters for one of the large estates that line the upper south side of Dorset Street. The house on the south side that housed servants across the road has been turned into a day spa. The original idea was to turn it into a bed and breakfast as I understand. However, the idea of a spa came into being during renovations. Supposedly the work crew couldn't stand the noises and screaming they heard.

My brother-in-law, Stacy, used to cut grass on an adjoining property. He says that he always found he made himself go faster when cutting the portion of the lawn between the two houses. He says things just don't feel right there. He didn't know about the supposed hauntings at the time.

Later Stacy met a person, through the drummer in his band, that is believed to have seen the ghosts haunting the house on Dorset. He will say very little about what he saw except to say that what is in there is very real. Stacy recounted in front of this person that he heard the ghost appears at the bottom of the basement stairway holding the heads of two young children. The ghost is also rumoured to travel toward the person seeing the apparition.

The Haunted School in Whitby—

A friend of mine works at a school in Whitby. She is a believer in spirits and the supernatural. She believes there are at least two ghosts, maybe three, residing in the school. Her husband also believes this. He says he gets a strange feeling sometimes when he picks her up from the school.

Some of the children have seen the ghosts, according to my friend. One day two little girls sent a chill into their teacher. Most of the children were out at recess when one of the girls asked the teacher, "Who is that lady standing next to you?"

The teacher looked over and saw no one there. She asked what the girl was talking about.

The girl spoke up, "Yes, there she is and she's wearing a really pretty dress."

Children are sometimes excited because ghosts are helping them at the chalk board or playing with them by moving the chalk around. These ghosts seem friendly and even playful.

There is supposed to be another presence in the basement. Not a nice one. My friend asked her husband to accompany her down to the storage area in the basement to get some supplies for her classroom the next day. She will not go into the basement alone if at all possible. He says he understands why; the feeling is creepy. She will buy supplies that she could otherwise get for free so long as it allows her to avoid the basement.

Dan Araujo

Haunted Cottage in Bowmanville

Dear Mr. Boyle:

I have a story to tell, which I have never been able to forget. My husband and I bought a cottage back in 1996. It was on Lake Ontario in the town of Bowmanville, Ontario. The house was in bad need of repair and we did a lot of work on it. We started by replacing the windows.

It was a bright sunny day when I arrived home after work. My husband met me at the door and noticed that my blood sugars were low. I am diabetic. I was given a glass of juice and was sitting on the couch in front of the large window that looks over the lake.

I was sharing my day with my husband when I caught what I thought at the time was the reflection of a man walking past the window. He was wearing a plaid shirt and coveralls. Just what an old-fashioned farmer would wear. I stopped in mid-sentence and was surprised when my husband said he did not see the man. I went out onto the deck where the man had to have walked in order for him to pass the window.

You see, I really saw him in the mirrors that were on the wall I was facing. This meant that he was actually in the house when I saw him. I was shaken from the experience and started to cry. I blamed it on my low blood sugar and dismissed it. I saw my neighbour a short time later and was telling him of my experience and he said that this had been farm land at one time.

Over the period we lived in the house, whenever my blood sugars were low, I would feel a presence in the bedroom at the back of the house. I would be ironing, and could swear that someone was in the room with me. I would turn around and no one was there. Or I would be sleeping and would awaken, feeling the weight of someone sitting on the bed. Most of the time it would be when my husband was working nights. It frightened me.

The last time this happened to me was the year my step-daughter got married. We had also sold the house and were packing up and getting ready for the wedding. We had a garden party the day after the wedding and it was bright and sunny. We were in and out of the house and the guests were outside under tents set up on the property.

The party was winding down and there were only a few guests left when I felt I needed some juice. I went into the house. I was coming out of the bathroom when I looked across the hall into the spare room that *was full of boxes. There, bending over one of the boxes, was a lady in a long black dress. She looked up at me as I came through the door, but she seemed to look through me, as though I was not there. I stood there, just staring at her. I came out to where my guests were and they knew something had happened. I told them what I had seen and I started to cry. They were certain that I was upset and very frightened, but I think they had a hard time believing me.*

I know what I saw and what I have experienced since living in that house and I can't explain it. It was as though they wanted me to know they were there and maybe because we were changing things, this caused them to show themselves. I don't know.

For some strange reason I was able to feel and see things only when my blood sugars were low and only when I lived in that house. It has been two years now since we moved and I have had low blood sugar episodes since, but no ghostly encounters.

Readers Name Withheld by Request

Haunted House, Etobicoke

Dear Mr. Boyle:

A friend has just recently introduced me to one of your books. I was quickly captivated and read it in a day. Then I read it again.

My friend, Laura, who actually gave me two of your books, has known me for about twenty-five years. We've been early childhood friends. We grew up one block from each other. Laura knows about the house I grew up in. She never liked it much. We'd usually play at her house.

You see, not a day went by without an incident in my house. It was typical to see plants moving and the television would go off and on. The lights did the same thing. We heard footsteps, loud and clear. There were doors that shut, or muffled voices, and most often our stuff would simply disappear! Small things, but not very often would they re-appear. I always said that one day we would find all our missing belongings stashed away somewhere in that house. Of course, we never did.

My brothers, being older, were scared, but tried not to show it. I kept a diary for two solid years, until one day even it went missing.

We never really felt alone in that house. We children would discuss it among ourselves. Dad wouldn't hear of it. Mom would just say we were imagining things.

The basement was the worst. Our cats would not go down there. If we made them they would freeze with their backs hunched up and their hair on end.

Once we accidentally shut the basement door with one cat downstairs. It went missing all day. At night we were in the basement because we could hear her meowing. We eventually found her between the ceiling and the floor, above our heads. We could not figure that one out.

My birthday is in June and when I was little my Mom would have a pool party for me. All my friends were there. One year, one of my friends went downstairs through the side door to use the washroom. She came up right away, crying and screaming. She wanted my Mom to call her Mom to come and take her home.

Even though all kinds of strange things happened there we never knew the extent of it until my parents finally sold the house.

On that day my Mother arrived and took my husband and me out to dinner. She started off by saying, "You know how you kids always thought the house was haunted? So I lied! It really was haunted and the first time I saw the ghost I almost died. I thought we were being robbed."

She finally told us what she had seen. It was very late at night and Mom and Dad were in bed. Dad was asleep and Mom was reading. Suddenly a man came into the bedroom. My Mom froze. She knew Dad was snoring and couldn't do a thing. She thought they were being robbed. So she pretended she was sleeping, too, and hoped he wouldn't hurt anyone. He seemed so real. My Mom blinked a little and slowly opened her eyes. He faded away.

My Mom told me about all the different times she would see him. He would be sitting on the porch when she got home from work. She would see him in the hallway or downstairs or in the laundry room.

My old house is haunted. I truly believe it now. The strange part, though, is our neighbours had strange occurrences in their houses, too. My childhood friend, Cindy, who lived next door, said her Mom felt the same way about their home. I only found this out last week.

Cindy told me that, as a child, she heard the voices of English-accented women having a tea party. This was heard only on weekends. Crosses would appear in the windows.

We also remembered another house on the street that was rumoured to be haunted. Could our whole street have been haunted?

Dana Gallant

Ghosts of World War I

Dear Mr. Boyle:

You say in your books that when you enter certain areas you can almost feel a presence. For me, in many ways, this is an everyday occurrence. Not the seeing of things, but the feeling of things.

Everyone in my family is either able to see or feel the unknown. Then there are the family members who can do both. There have been experiences reported by family members for over a hundred years. My Grandfather had them. When he was little, during the First World War, he woke up to find a headless soldier at the foot of his bed. The headless soldier turned out to be his uncle, who was away at war. His uncle appeared to him at the exact moment of his death.

My other Grandfather had an experience when my Mom was about five years old. He came running out of his bedroom crying, "Annie help me, they're coming through the walls after me."

My Grandfather had been a sniper in the First World War. What I believe he saw were the men he had killed. My Grandmother simply walked into their room and said a prayer of absolution, banishing all that was not of God from their room. After that my Grandfather was able to sleep without the nightmares that had plagued him since the war.

May Cuing

Dead Son Returns

Dear Mr. Boyle:

I found your book HAUNTED ONTARIO in my local public library. I made the mistake of reading it when my kids were asleep and my husband was out. I enjoyed the depth of your research and the way it was presented. It did, however, scare the bejeepers out of me.

Since I enjoyed your book so much I decided to write you with my own story.

My own story requires a bit of background so please bear with me. I grew up in a neighbourhood in south Ottawa. At the age of ten I acquired a paper route. I delivered the Ottawa Citizen newspaper for about four years. I was also playing hockey at the time and most of my "paper" money went to the costs of hockey. Every two weeks I was required to collect money owing to the Citizen from my customers. Hockey also gave out raffle tickets to each player to try to sell, also to make the cost less for parents.

I naturally asked my customers to support my hockey and they gave generously over the years. One year it seemed that I had a lot of raffle tickets to sell and since I was getting tired of asking my customers I decided to try a different street.

I was about 13 years old and it was on a Wednesday night that I rang the doorbell of a particular house. "Good evening, my name is Heidi Metcalfe and I was wondering if you would like to support my hockey team by buying a raffle ticket?"

The gentleman looked about thirty, clean shaven, friendly and about 5'8" Light hair, a sweater and a pair of blue jeans. He told me that his parents were out of town but would be back the next Wednesday. He said that they always supported minor hockey teams and would certainly buy a ticket. I thanked him and went on my way.

Having some experience in selling raffle tickets I went back the following Wednesday. A gentleman about fifty or sixty answered the door. He looked almost like the gentleman of a week before only older. I told him that I was there last week and what must have been his son told me to come back this night.

He didn't say anything at first and then said that I must be mistaken. I described the man of a week before and told him that he said his parents were out of town but to come in a week. He turned really pale and said that he was at his son's funeral the week before.

I was shocked and I apologized. I went straight home after that and did not bother that family anymore.

Sincerely,
Heidi Metcalfe

Visitor Information

The Albion Hotel
P.O. Box 114,
Bayfield, Ontario
N0M 1G0
519-565-2641
albion@cabletv.on.ca

Blinkbonnie Harbour Inn
50 Main Street,
Gananoque, Ontario
K7G 2L7
613-382-7272
800-265-7474

Emma's Back Porch
2084 Old Lakeside Rd.,
Burlington, Ontario
L7R 1A3
905-634-2084
kalin@emma'sbackporch.ca

Fort George
Superintendent
Niagara National Historic Sites
Box 787
Niagara-on-the-Lake, Ontario
L0S 1J0
905-465-4257
Kyle Upton-Ghost Tours of Fort George
ghosttours@hotmail.com

Grafton Village Inn
10830 Country Rd. 2
Grafton, Ontario
K0K 2G0
905-349-3024
info@graftonvillage.com

Gravenhurst Opera House
295 Muskoka Road South
Gravenhurst, Ontario
P1P 1J1
705 687-5550
888-495-8888
rcarling@gravenhurst.net

Yesterdays Resort
Highway 69A
French River Station, Ontario
P0M 1A0
705-857-3383
800-663-3383

Bibliography

Chandler, Charlotte, Nobody's Perfect: Billy Wilder A Personal Biography (Simon & Shuster, 2002)

Cochrane, Hugh, Gateway to Oblivion, (Doubleday & Company, 1980)

Colombo, John Robert, Haunted Toronto (Hounslow Press, 1996)

Crowe, Cameron, Comversations with Wilder (Alfred A Knopf, 1999)

Brambilla, G. et al, Marilyn Monroe (Rizzoli New York, 1995)

Guiles, Fred Lawrence, Legend (Scarborough House Pulishers, 1991)

Harvey, James, Movie Love in the Fifties (Alfred A Knopf, 2001)

Hawke's William, Gananoque, (1974)

Kael, Pauline, For Keeps: 30 Years at the Movies (Dutton, 1994)

Lally,Kevin, Wilder Times: The Life of Billy Wilder (Henry Holt, 1996)

Leaming, Barbara, Marilyn Monroe, (Three Rivers Press, 1998)

Lidgold, Carole, The Guild Inn, (Brookrodge Publishing House, 2000)

Mady, Najla, BOO! (Esprit International Communications, 1993)

Miller, Arthur & Toubiana, Serge, The Misfits: Story of a Shoot (Phaidon)

Petry, Bob, Bala (Lynx Images, 1998)

Statford, J.P., The Many Stages of Our Lives (Gravenhurst Opera House, 2001)

Turcette, Dorothy, Burlington (The Burlington Historical Society, 1992)

Upton, Kyle, Niagra's Ghosts at Fort George (Kyle Upton, 1999)

Victor, Adam, The Marilyn Encyclopedia (Overlook Press, 1999)

Newspapers

Fragomeni, Carmela, *The Hamilton Spectator*, Halloween Busy for Canada's "top ghost hunter', October 31, 2001

Zuzyk, Ron, *The Burlington Post*, Burlington hotbed of supernatural phenomenon, March, 2000

The Goderich Signal, November 11, 1987

Magazines

Cruickshank, Tom, The Best of Bayfield, *Century Home*, June-July 1992.

Index

All photographs: Terry Boyle's Collection
except:
p. 116, 118, 120 provided by the Gananoque Historical Society